Growing On Your Way to Heaven!
Getting Started In
Your Christian Life

Dr. Norman P. Anderson

© Copyright 2004 Norman P. Anderson. All rights reserved.

No part of this publication may be reproduced, stored in a retrieval system, or transmitted, in any form or by any means, electronic, mechanical, photocopying, recording, or otherwise, without the written prior permission of the author.

Printed in Victoria, Canada

Note for Librarians: a cataloguing record for this book that includes Dewey Classification and US Library of Congress numbers is available from the National Library of Canada. The complete cataloguing record can be obtained from the National Library's online database at: www.nlc-bnc.ca/amicus/index-e.html

ISBN 14120-2024-7

TRAFFORD

This book was published *on-demand* in cooperation with Trafford Publishing. On-demand publishing is a unique process and service of making a book available for retail sale to the public taking advantage of on-demand manufacturing and Internet marketing. **On-demand publishing** includes promotion, retail sales, manufacturing, order fulfilment, accounting and collecting royalties on behalf of the author.

Suite 6E, 2333 Government St., Victoria, B.C. V8T 4P4, CANADA
Phone   250-383-6864   Toll-free   1-888-232-4444 (Canada & US)
Fax   250-383-6804   E-mail   sales@trafford.com
Web site   www.trafford.com   TRAFFORD PUBLISHING IS A DIVISION OF TRAFFORD HOLDINGS LTD.
Trafford Catalogue #03-2603   www.trafford.com/robots/03-2603.html

10   9   8   7   6   5   4   3   2   1

Table of Contents

Introduction . . . . Page 3

Chapter 1   What Has Happened To Me? . . . . Page 6

Chapter 2   How Long Will It Last? . . . . Page 15

Chapter 3   When I Sin, What Do I Do? . . . . Page 25

Chapter 4   The Word Of God In Your Life! . . . . Page 38

Chapter 5   Prayer - Developing Intimacy With God! . . . Page 49

Chapter 6   The Church of Jesus Christ! . . . . Page 61

Chapter 7   Baptism - Your Public Proclamation of Faith! Page 79

Chapter 8   The Lord's Supper: Remembering Our Lord!   Page 91

Chapter 9   Holy Living In An Unholy World . . . . Page 100

Chapter 10   If God Loves Me, Why Does He Allow Me
To Suffer? . . . . Page 118

Chapter 11   The Holy Spirit In Your Life . . . . Page 130

Chapter 12   You Are A Manager For The Lord! . . . . . . Page 142

Chapter 13   Your Life's Purpose Until You Arrive Home! . . Page 158

Acknowledgements

All of the Scripture references used in this book are taken from the New King James translation. Copyright @ 1979, 1980, 1982 by Thomas Nelson, Inc. Used by permission. All rights reserved.

I dedicate this book to my four children and my grandchildren. I express deep gratitude to my Lord and Savior, Jesus Christ, for the faith of my four children. They all love the Lord Jesus and are endeavoring to serve Him. It is my prayer that each of my grandchildren will experience a true new birth in Jesus Christ and that each one of them will seek to grow obediently in the Lord. Arriving in heaven and finding them all there with me someday will be provide unmeasured joy.

I'm very grateful for the editing work of a dear friend, Florence Jacobson. As she did for my first book, she has helped me immensely to communicate more precisely and with greater clarity.

While I give credit to direct quotes used in this book, there is nothing really original with me. My life has been greatly molded by many professors, pastoral colleagues and friends too numerous to mention. I owe a deep debt of gratitude to all of these wonderful people who have crossed my pathway by the providence of our God. While this book comes from my mind and my heart dedicated to my Savior and Lord, Jesus Christ, it is fashioned by my journey with many fellow travelers.

Introduction

This book is a sequel to my book "So You Want To Go To Heaven! God Tells You How!" My previous book tells you how you can have a personal relationship with God through Jesus Christ, God's Son. It tells you what God says in the Bible about being sure you will arrive in heaven as your life on earth ends. This book is for you as a new believer in Jesus Christ. It is designed to guide you through the Bible to become an obedient follower of Jesus Christ while you are on your journey to heaven.

When you trusted Christ personally as Savior and Lord, you were born from above or "born again." Jesus used this terminology when He was speaking to Nicodemus in John 3:3-5. This means that God has made you alive spiritually and given you eternal life as a free gift. Christ has fulfilled His promise to come and live within you spiritually as the resurrected Christ.

God wants every one of His children to grow to maturity. Jesus said in Matthew 5:48, *"Be perfect, therefore, as your heavenly Father is perfect."* The word "perfect" means "mature." The goal is that each of us imperfect human beings will continue to mature until ultimately in heaven we will be completely perfect even as our Heavenly Father is perfect. We are to be in this growth pattern throughout our earthly pilgrimage, continually becoming more like our Savior and Lord, Jesus Christ.

If you do not already have a Bible, it is important to get one. One of the modern translations will be easier to read than the King James Version which was translated almost four centuries ago. There is a New King James Version which has attempted to update the archaic expressions of the King James Version. Another very readable and reliable translation is the New International Version. The recently done new Living Bible Translation is also easy to understand.

Reading the Bible is far more important than reading this book. However, this book is intended to guide you in the basic teachings of the Bible that are needed especially by new Christians. By looking up the references in your own Bible you will become acquainted with the Bible.

You are a new baby in Christ. Now you should begin to grow. How do you do this? 1 Peter 2:2-3 tells us: *"Like newborn babies, crave pure spiritual milk, so that by it you may grow up in your salvation, now that you have tasted that the Lord is good."*

The Word of God is filled with spiritual milk and also with meat. The milk will help you grow until you are able to digest the meat. This book will give you the milk, the basics for walking with the Lord Jesus in day by day, moment by moment, intimate fellowship. It is designed to get you started growing so that you might learn to obey Christ in your life here on earth.

This book will also begin to give you some spiritual meat that you might mature in your faith. The meat of Scripture deals with deeper teachings about God and His eternal plan for us. The writer of Hebrews scolds some of his readers for not growing to the point of being able to digest solid food. In Hebrews 5:12-15, we read:

> *For though by this time you ought to be teachers, you need someone to teach you again the first principles of the oracles of God; and you have come to need milk and not solid food. For everyone who partakes only of milk is unskilled in the word of righteousness, for he is a babe. But solid food belongs to those who are of full age, that is, those who by reason of use have their senses exercised to discern both good and evil.*

Growing up in Christ is a life time process! So don't get discouraged if it seems you are growing slowly. Keep reading the Word of God and trusting Christ Jesus in every situation. Physical growth is imperceptible from day to day, but over a few months and years, growth becomes obvious. So it is with following Jesus Christ. Persist in following Him obediently and you will grow up in Him.

It is not enough to master these basic teachings of Scripture in your mind; it is God's will that you live them out in your life. At the end of each chapter there are some study questions to help you grasp the truths of Scripture, and then obey them. Jesus taught that the growth process for His new disciples (followers) involves *"teaching them to obey everything I have commanded you,"* (Matthew 28:20).

The apostle Paul expressed the purpose of his ministry in terms of people not programs. In Colossians 1:28-29, he wrote, *"We proclaim him, admonishing and teaching everyone with all wisdom, so that we present everyone perfect (or mature) in Christ. To this end I labor, struggling with all this energy, which so powerfully works in me."* Just as the apostle Paul proclaimed, admonished and taught everyone so that they would mature in Christ, so this book is designed to help you mature in your faith and in your daily walk with Christ Jesus.

Enjoy the journey as you follow Jesus Christ and grow in Him.

Chapter One

What Has Happened To Me?

A party in heaven

You repented from your sin and turned to Jesus Christ as your Savior. You ceased depending upon your own good works to make you right with God. You trusted Christ's death on the cross in your place as the only means of being accepted by God, the Father. You received Christ Jesus into your life as Savior and Lord and the angels in heaven threw a party.

In a sense, it was your birthday party! They were celebrating that another sinner was cleansed by Christ's blood and was now saved from hell. They were rejoicing that another sinner was now God's redeemed child. Take out your Bible and read Luke 15. There Jesus told three parables about lost people. The parable of the lost sheep, the parable of the lost coin and the parable of the lost son are all about lost sinners who find their way back to God, the Father.

In each of these parables there is rejoicing in heaven.[1] For example, verse 10 says, *"In the same way, I tell you, there is rejoicing in the presence of the angels of God over one sinner who repents."* In the third story, when the lost son returns to the father, the father is anxiously awaiting his return. He spots him coming when he is still a long way off. Overcome with love for him, he runs to meet him, throws his arms around him and kisses him. He provides him with the best robe, a ring for his finger and sandals for his feet. He prepares the best feast to celebrate that his son has come home.

Let it sink into your heart and mind! The prodigal, the lost son, is you! You were hopelessly lost in your sins, destined for hell. God in His love reached you and drew you to Himself. He sacrificed His own Son, Jesus Christ, on the cross in your place so that He might forgive your sins and give you the free gift of eternal life. He saw that you heard this good news of His grace. You repented and came as a sinner to accept what the Father did for you. Instead of your old tattered, dirty garments of sin, you

---

1   A parable is a story that is told to teach a spiritual truth.

now have a robe of righteousness given to you. God sees you as righteous because His Son, Jesus Christ, is righteous and He has given to you His righteousness in place of your old rags of sin. So a party has taken place in heaven!

The angels are rejoicing over your salvation.

Your name recorded in heaven

God keeps a careful record of the names of all those who have repented and trusted Christ Jesus as their Savior. He writes their names in His book of life. The moment that you trusted Christ Jesus as your Savior and Lord, God wrote your name in His book of life.

Read Revelation 20:11-15. This passage tells us about the final judgment of unbelievers. Only *unbelievers* will be there. As you read this passage of Scripture, you will notice that the book of life is opened. In verse 15 we read *"If anyone's name was not found written in the book of life, he was thrown into the lake of fire."* Eternal punishment awaits the unbeliever.

In Luke 10, we find Jesus sending out His followers to do his work in the cities and towns of Israel. When they return, they are excited about all that they have seen accomplished. In verse 17, we read, *"The seventy-two returned with joy and said, 'Lord, even the demons submit to us in your name.'"* Jesus put everything in proper perspective as He told them: *"do not rejoice that the spirits submit to you, but rejoice that your names are written in heaven"* (verse 20). Before reading further, stop and thank God that He has written your name in His book of life.

Born into God's family

Jesus used the words *"born again"* or *"born from above"* when He was speaking to Nicodemus in John 3. The only way that a person can see God's kingdom is by being *"born again."*[2] He was speaking about the experience of being born spiritually into God's family. Jesus was comparing the experience of being born again spiritually into God's family with the physical birth when you were born into your earthly family. Verse 6 says, *"Flesh gives*

---

2   John 3:3,5

birth to flesh but the Spirit gives birth to spirit." At the moment you trusted Christ Jesus by faith to save you from your sins, you were born into God's spiritual family.

The apostle Peter[3] wrote of this experience in 1 Peter 1:22-23:

> *Now that you have purified yourselves by obeying the truth so that you have sincere love for your brothers, love one another deeply, from the heart. For you have been born again, not of perishable seed, but of imperishable, through the living and enduring word of God.*

As a new Christian you are born into the eternal family of God's redeemed people,[4] not by a human father's seed which is perishable, but by the imperishable seed of God through His word. This new relationship comes about only by what God has done for you in response to your repentance and faith in Christ. You now have spiritual brothers and sisters. Every true believer, who has repented and trusted Christ as you have done, is your brother and sister in Christ.

1 John 3:1-2 speaks of this new relationship in God's family.

> *How great is the love the Father has lavished on us, that we should be called children of God! And that is what we are! The reason the world does not know us is that it did not know him. Dear friends, now we are children of God, and what we will be has not yet been made known. But we know that when he appears, we shall be like him, for we shall see him as he is.*

---

[3] Peter was a fisherman when Jesus called him to be one of twelve disciples. He was chosen to be one of Jesus' apostles upon whom He founded his church. Peter wrote two letters near the end of the New Testament called 1 and 2 Peter.

[4] The concept of redemption or redeemed is referred to often in the New Testament. It speaks of Jesus paying the price of our sin so that we might be set free from the penalty of our sin required by God's absolute righteousness. It is much like a slave being purchased at the slave auction by a benevolent owner in order to grant the slave his freedom.

In 2 Corinthians 6:16-18, the apostle Paul[5] wrote about the wonderful promise of God to call us His children and to have us call Him, our Father.

> . . . *For we are the temple of the living God. As God has said: "I will live among them, and I will be their God, and they will be my people." "Therefore come out from them and be separate, says the Lord. Touch no unclean thing, and I will receive you." "I will be a Father to you, and you will be my sons and daughters, says the Lord Almighty."*

In Romans 8:15, as Paul wrote about the Holy Spirit in our lives, he said,

> *For you did not receive a spirit that makes you a slave again to fear, but you received the Spirit of sonship. And by him we cry, "Abba,[6] Father."*

Bathe your heart and mind with the words of the Psalmist David in Psalm 103:8-14:

> *The LORD is compassionate and gracious, slow to anger, abounding in love. He will not always accuse nor will he harbor his anger forever; he does not treat us as our sins deserve or repay us according to our iniquities. For as high as the heavens are above the earth, so great is his love for those who fear him; as far as the east is from the west, so far has he removed our transgressions from us. As a father has compassion on his children, so the LORD has compassion on those who fear him; for he knows how we are formed, he remembers that we are dust.*

Did you have the experience of being born into a good family physically? Did you know the love of a father and mother who truly sought to care for you and nurture you? Then you can

---

[5] The apostle Paul was formerly an enemy of Jesus who pursued followers of Jesus to persecute them and even put them to death. You can read about Jesus confronting Saul (his previous name) in Acts 9. He was completely changed by Jesus Christ and became one of Jesus' apostles who wrote much of the New Testament.

[6] "Abba" is an Aramaic word meaning "Father." It is a very personal, intimate word like saying "daddy."

identify with God's love for you that makes you His dear child. You don't have to earn His compassion and love by your behavior. But maybe you did not have that experience with your earthly father. You had to earn his love. The word "father" may not bring good memories. If so, your heavenly Father is different. You can rest in His love without having to earn it by your behavior. God the Father accepts you completely and unconditionally because of His Son, Jesus Christ. You can believe this because God tells the truth.

A brand new person in Christ

Paul, the apostle, wrote to the Corinthian church in 2 Corinthians 5:17: *"Therefore, if anyone is in Christ, he is a new creation; the old has gone, the new has come!"* He doesn't mean that you are suddenly perfect and will never sin anymore. He means that God has entered into your life and performed a miracle, changing you into a different person. God has placed you in Christ. That means when God the Father looks at you, He looks at you as being righteous like His Son. That is what the Bible means when it speaks about us being justified in God's sight.

Christ has taken up His residence in your life through His Holy Spirit. You have been reconciled to God, that is, you are no longer His enemy but you are His child who is at peace with Him. He has made you alive to Him and alive to His Word. You will read the Bible now and find that it begins to make sense like it did not before. You are given the Holy Spirit of God who gives you new desires and new joy – indeed, new life! Before you trusted Christ, you were dead spiritually; now you are alive spiritually. Before you had no interest in learning about God; now you have started to sense an expanding inner desire to learn more and more about our wonderful God. Previous to trusting Christ, you did not care if you sinned against God; now there is a growing longing to please Him who has done so much for you.

The Holy Spirit lives in you

In John 3:5 Jesus said to Nicodemus: *"I tell you the truth, no one can enter the kingdom of God unless he is born of water and the Spirit."* To understand what Jesus meant by the "water" birth and the "Spirit" birth, you need simply to read the next verse. He is comparing the physical birth (the water birth) that brought you into this world alive with the spiritual birth (Spirit birth). So the Holy Spirit came into your life when you trusted Christ Jesus as your Savior and Lord.

This initial coming of the Holy Spirit into your life is known as the baptism of the Holy Spirit. Some Christians teach that the baptism of the Holy Spirit comes at a later time in the believer's life. However, as you carefully study the New Testament Scriptures, you will see that in order to be a Christian, the Holy Spirit must baptize you. 1 Corinthians 12:13 says: *"For we are all baptized by one Spirit into one body - whether Jews or Greeks, slave or free - and we were all given the one Spirit to drink."*

By the term "one body," the apostle Paul is speaking of the church universal, the true church of Jesus Christ that is made up of all who have truly repented and believed in Jesus Christ. This body of believers crosses all denominational boundaries. Every truly repentant believer in Jesus Christ is a member of the universal church of Jesus Christ. So, if you are a member of the universal church of Jesus Christ, you got there by being "baptized by the one Spirit" of God. In Romans 8:9, Paul, the apostle, makes it very clear that you are not even one who belongs to Christ unless the Holy Spirit lives in you. *"You, however, are controlled not by the sinful nature but by the Spirit, if the Spirit of God lives in you. And if anyone does not have the Spirit of God, he does not belong to Christ."*

We will study much more about the Holy Spirit in chapter eleven of this book. For now, rejoice that God's Holy Spirit is in you and He will begin teaching you the Bible as you read and study it. This is one of the primary reasons that Jesus sent His Holy Spirit into the hearts of His followers. In John 14:26 we read the words of Jesus to His disciples: *"But the Counselor, the Holy Spirit, whom the Father will send in my name, will teach you all things and remind you of everything I have said to you."*

You are now a member of Christ's kingdom

The apostle Paul wrote to the church that had come into existence in a city called Colosse. In Colossians 1:13-14 we read: *"For he has rescued us from the dominion of darkness and brought us into the kingdom of the Son he loves, in whom we have redemption and the forgiveness of sins."* When you read the previous verses, you will see that Paul is speaking about what the Heavenly Father has done for you as you trusted Jesus Christ as your Savior and Lord. He has redeemed or bought you with the price of His son's death. You no longer belong to Satan who rules over the dominion of darkness. You have been transferred into the kingdom of the Son, Jesus Christ which is *"the kingdom of light."*[7] Before you trusted Christ Jesus you walked in darkness. Now you walk in the light of Jesus Christ and in the light of His truth. You are a citizen of heaven even though you are still a resident of this world.

As a citizen of the kingdom of Christ, your sins are forgiven. To "forgive" literally means to remove the debt or to send the debt away. Jesus Christ paid the debt that you could not pay. He died in your place as He took the debt for your sins upon Himself. He paid your penalty and now your debt is completely removed from you. You are no longer held accountable for your sins. Psalm 103:12 says *"as far as the east is from the west, so far has he removed our transgressions from us."* Think about the meaning of this. The Psalmist did not say "north and south" but "east and west." If you go north and pass the North Pole, you will immediately be going south. North and south can be measured. When you go west or east, you will keep going west or east; your direction never changes until you turn completely around. You cannot measure east from west and that is how far God has removed your sins from you. They are never again to be brought up against you. You are free from the judgment of God against your sin. You are redeemed and you are forgiven as a citizen of God's kingdom.

You are a saint

Perhaps it will startle you, that God calls you a "saint." Every true believer is called a "saint."

Paul the apostle frequently addressed the people to whom he wrote as saints.[8] Even in the Old Testament, God's people are often referred to as saints.[9]

---

[7] Colossians 1:12

[8] 2 Corinthians 1:1; Ephesians 1:1; Philippians 1:1; etc.

The word "saint" in the New Testament is translated from a Greek[10] word that means "holy one." The same root word in its verb form is translated in several places as "sanctified" or in some of the modern translations, it may be expressed by words like "set apart for God's holy purposes." The term "saint" is used of every true believer to speak about our position that we now have before God through Jesus Christ our Savior. God, the Father, sees us as His holy people because He sees us through the holiness and righteousness of His Son, Jesus Christ. It is our standing before God the minute that we receive Jesus Christ into our lives. We are no longer regarded as "sinners" but we are now regarded as "saints" in God's eyes because of Jesus Christ. Paul the apostle wrote to the Colossian church in Colossians 1:12: ". . . *giving thanks to the Father, who has qualified you to share in the inheritance of the saints in the kingdom of light."* You and I are qualified to be called saints only because Jesus Christ is our Savior. What a great honor God has bestowed upon us that He calls us "saints."

As saints, we are also sanctified or set apart for God's holy use. As saints, we are to be growing more and more like our holy Savior, Jesus Christ. We do not belong to ourselves any longer. We belong to Christ and are temples of the Holy Spirit. To the Corinthian church, Paul, the apostle, wrote:

> *. . . do you not know that your body is the temple of the Holy Spirit who is in you, whom you have from God, and you are not your own? For you were bought at a price; therefore glorify God in your body and in your spirit, which are God's (1 Corinthians 6:19-20).*

One of the traditional Christian denominations teaches that saints are particularly godly people who are canonized by the church. To qualify to be a saint, one has to be dead for a considerable period of time, have lived an exceptionally holy life and have performed at least one miracle that has been authenticated by the church. This definition of "saint" is not found in the Bible.

---

[9] 1 Samuel 2:9; Psalm 16:3; Psalm 30:4; Psalm 31:23; Psalm 34:9; Psalm 116:15; Psalm 149:1,4-5,9; etc.

[10] The New Testament was written in Greek, the common trade language used in Jesus' day in the Middle Eastern region.

You are blessed with many spiritual blessings

We could go on listing many more blessings from God that you now possess as a child of God. The apostle Paul expresses this thought in Ephesians 1:3 where he wrote: *"Praise be to the God and Father of our Lord Jesus Christ who has blessed us in the heavenly realms with every spiritual blessing in Christ."* Read on in the first chapter of Ephesians and you will find many other spiritual blessings that every believer possesses in Christ Jesus. This is true of many parts of the Bible. You will discover blessing after blessing that you now have as a result of being one of God's redeemed children. Whenever God shows you a blessing He has given you in Christ Jesus, take the time to thank Him and to praise Him.

Some study questions for your reflection

1. When you study Luke 15, what does the rejoicing in heaven tell us about God's nature?
2. What is the qualification for having your name written in God's book of life?
3. What did Jesus mean by being "born again"? Do you know for sure that you are "born again" into God's family?
4. 2 Corinthians 5:17 teaches that when you are in Christ, you are a new creation. Does that mean that you are perfect and will never sin anymore? If not, what does it mean that you are a new creature?
5. As a new believer, where is the Holy Spirit in relationship to your life?
6. According to Colossians 1:13-14, what has Christ done for you when you trusted Him as your Savior and Lord?
7. Now that you have trusted Christ, God calls you a saint. What does it mean to be a "saint"?

Chapter Two

How Long Will It Last?

When you have trusted Christ as your Savior, you no longer belong to the dominion of darkness and Satan is no longer your master. Christ Jesus has entered your life and He has given you the gift of eternal life. Romans 6:23 says, *"For the wages of sin is death but the gift of God is eternal life in Jesus Christ, our Lord."* You may be asking, "So is this new life going to last? How long will this new relationship with God be mine"?

God wants you to have assurance that His gift of life and your relationship with Him will last forever. After all, "eternal life" is eternal, not just for a week or a month! He doesn't want you going through your life time not knowing for sure that you are right with Him and that you are on the way to heaven. He doesn't want you always to be wondering if you will be welcomed into heaven or if you will end up in hell.

False confidence or true confidence

On the other hand, there could be nothing worse than believing that you are right with God and on your way to heaven, only to find out that you have been deceived. God wants you to know that you have a genuine relationship with Him! He wants you to know Him in such a way that you know your salvation is real – not simply an imitation or counterfeit.

Satan holds many people in the deception of false assurance. Most people who believe they are right with God and that they will get to heaven base their faith in what they are trying to do for God. They believe that their good deeds will earn eternal life. This is a false assurance, one of the primary ways Satan deceives people. The Bible clearly teaches that heaven is achieved only by the grace of God, not by your works. It is totally a gift of God in response to your repentance and faith in Jesus Christ and His atoning death on the cross for you. Are you still depending in any way upon your goodness to get you to heaven? If so, then you are not saved from your sins and you are not born again by God's Spirit. Go back to Ephesians 2:8-9 and rethink what the Bible says about being saved by God's grace alone through faith alone in Jesus Christ alone. *"For it is by grace you have been saved, through faith - and this is not from yourselves, it is the gift of God - not by works, so that no one can boast."* [11]

There are also many people who claim to be born again but never show any evidence of new life in Christ. Because they prayed at some point in their lives, asking Jesus to forgive their sins, they assume that they are now saved and are going to go to heaven. Perhaps some well meaning Christian unwisely counseled them that they are going to heaven now, because they prayed "the sinner's prayer." Just going through the formality of praying a prayer, or being baptized, or any other kind of religious exercise, does not bring genuine new life in Christ. If there is no genuine repentance, then they are not born again.

Years ago, as I was the pastor of a small church, I heard of a young man who was living a wild sinful life. Supposedly he had accepted Christ as his Savior, but he was never involved in worship services or Bible studies. When I made contact with him, he said, "Well, it doesn't really matter how I live. Jesus forgives me for my sin, so I can do anything I wish and He will forgive me." Wrong!

If you have prayed to ask Jesus Christ to come into your life, but you have no intention of being His follower, then Christ will not enter your life, nor grant you new life. If all you desire is to live in your old sinful ways but to have God let you into heaven when you die, then you have not actually repented toward God. Repentance is turning from your own independence and your own sin to trust Christ and follow Him as your personal Savior and Lord.[12] God accepts you just as you are, when you come to Him in true repentance and faith, but it is not God's will to leave you that way. He wants to deliver you not only from the penalty of your sin but from the grip or power of your sin. Someday when He receives you into heaven, you will be free from the very presence of sin.

---

[11] If this is your condition, then you need to read my previous book, "So You Want To Go To Heaven! God Tells You How!" If you cannot locate it in a Christian bookstore, you may contact me. Write to me: Norman Anderson, 9619 E. Glencove Circle, Prescott Valley, AZ 86314.

[12] For a more complete understanding of the nature of repentance, see my previous book, So You Want To Go To Heaven, chapter 9.

So then, how can I know for sure that I have been born again?

The best evidence is that you see God working in your life. For example, you find yourself looking forward to attending church services. You begin to show concern for friends who are not believers in Jesus Christ. You are surprised by some of your attitudes that are changing. For you see, if Christ Jesus has truly entered your life, He has made you a new creation and your life will produce the good fruit of God's Spirit.

Therefore, here is a good question to ask: "Is there any fruit in my life"? If you have become alive in Christ, the Holy Spirit will begin to produce fruit through your changed heart.

Do not confuse the matter of having assurance by the good fruit in your life with gaining salvation by your own good works. They are two different things. You never can be saved from your sin and have Jesus Christ come into your life because of your good works or your good efforts. However, the good works and Christ-like fruit that you find in your life, after you have trusted Christ, give you assurance from God that Christ's presence in your life has made you alive.

Another way to understand it: good works before you accepted Christ don't earn your way to heaven; good works after you accepted Christ are expected evidence that you are truly following your Lord.

The fruit of the Spirit

The fruit that shows evidence that you have been born again is the fruit that comes from Christ through the Holy Spirit working in your life. Paul wrote about this fruit of the Spirit in Galatians 5:22-23. *"But the fruit of the Spirit is love, joy, peace, patience, kindness, goodness, faithfulness, gentleness and self control."* This is in stark contrast to the works of the old nature that Paul lists in the previous verses, Galatians 5:19-21.

The fruit of the Spirit is produced by the Spirit as you allow the Holy Spirit to control your life. His aim is to make you like Jesus Christ. Each item in this cluster of the Spirit's fruit is a characteristic of Christ Himself.

This fruit does not come by your self effort; it comes as you yield your life to the control of the Spirit. Take your Bible and read John 15:1-8. There you will see that Jesus teaches us that we are branches of the vine. He is the vine and we are to simply remain connected to the vine, so that we draw our life from the vine. As we do, the production of fruit is the automatic result of such a relationship with Him. The branches of a grape vine do not struggle to grow grapes. They just produce grapes as they remain connected to the vine. The key word is "remain."

What other kind of evidence?

The apostle John wrote a small letter to Christians in which he shares a number of tests by which we can know for sure that we have eternal life. He is not writing about things you must do in order to be saved; he is writing about the fruit or the evidence that we have truly been saved.

First, let us focus on 1 John 5:13 where John clarifies his purpose for his letter: *"I write these things to you who believe in the name of the Son of God so that you may know that you have eternal life."* Wonderful! That is exactly what you want to know, right? You want to be absolutely certain that you have eternal life.

Well, let's go back to the previous two verses where John wrote: *"And this is the testimony* (witness): *God has given us eternal life, and this life is in his Son. He who has the Son has life; he who does not have the Son of God does not have life."* Eternal life is all wrapped up in the person of Jesus Christ, God's Son. If you know that you have Christ Jesus living in you, then you know for sure that you have eternal life. So, how do you know that you have Jesus Christ living in you?

That is the reason John wrote his letter *"so that you may know that you have eternal life."*

John proposed at least six tests by which we can know that we have Jesus Christ in our lives.

- **Are you seeking to obey Christ's commands?**

1 John 2:3-6 says:

> *We know that we have come to know him if we obey his commands. The man who says, "I know him," but does not do what he commands is a liar, and the truth is not in him. But if anyone obeys his word, God's love is truly made complete in him: Whoever claims to live in him must walk as Jesus did.*

The word "obey" is a translation from the original text that means continually obeying or a pattern of obeying. It does not mean that we are not Christians if we occasionally sin or occasionally disobey through our weakness. (We will deal with the matter of the Christian and his sin in the next chapter.) What John is saying is that a person who truly knows Christ does not exhibit a pattern of constant disobedience to God's Word. Certainly, when there is no desire to obey Christ and no evidence of obedience to Christ, there is no new life in that person. John emphasizes the same truth in 1 John 2:29: *"If you know that he* (Jesus) *is righteous, you know that everyone who does* (is doing) *what is right has been born of him."*

- **Is your lifestyle a continual pattern of living in sin and darkness?**

The flip side of obedience is constantly living in sin. John deals with this matter of constantly sinning and yet professing to know Christ in 1 John 3:7-10:

> *Dear children,[13] do not let anyone lead you astray. He who does what is right is righteous, just as he* (Christ) *is righteous. He who does what is sinful is of the devil, because the devil has been sinning from the beginning. The reason the Son of God appeared was to destroy the devil's work. No one who is born of God will continue to sin, because God's seed remains in him; he cannot go on sinning, because he has been born of God. This is how we know who the children of God are and who the children of the devil are: Anyone who does not do what is right is not a child of God; nor is anyone who does not love his brother.*

---

[13] The word "children" is used by John to refer to those who are true believers and are therefore the children of God.

God does not want anyone to believe that he is truly born again and on his way to heaven when his life of continual, habitual sin denies his profession of faith. This is not talking about the occasional sin of the Christian; nor is it speaking about an enslaving habit over which you have not yet gained victory. It is speaking about a life that is continuing on in the same way as before you professed Christ Jesus as Savior and Lord. If the pattern is one of continually walking in darkness, that person's lifestyle speaks louder than his words. The reality is he is still a child of the devil.

- **Has God given you a love for your brothers?**

It is God's will for us as Christians to act lovingly toward all men, seeking to meet the needs of those around us. However, it is my view that when John speaks of loving your brothers, he is speaking specifically about loving other Christians. I John 3:14-15 says,

> *We know that we have passed from death to life, because we love our brothers. Anyone who does not love remains in death. Anyone who hates his brother is a murderer, and you know that no murderer has eternal life in him.*

Jesus warned His disciples in Matthew 5:21-22: *"You have heard that it was said to the people long ago, 'Do not murder, and anyone who murders will be subject to judgment.' But I tell you that anyone who is angry with his brother will be subject to judgment."* 1 John 2:9-10 says: *"Anyone who claims to be in the light but hates his brother is still in the darkness. Whoever loves his brother lives in the light, and there is nothing in him to make him stumble."*

Since you prayed to the Lord Jesus, repenting and trusting Him as your Savior and Lord, do you find a love in your heart for other Christians? Do you have a desire to be with your Christian brothers and sisters? Do you have love in your heart that causes you to want to share with those who are needy as God enables you? Is God giving you a heart of compassion and love for your fellow Christians? If this is happening in your life, this is clear evidence that Christ Jesus lives in you.

- **Do you know the witness of the Holy Spirit of God within your heart?**

In several places in John's letter, he teaches us about the Holy Spirit's work in the true believer's life. 1 John 3:24 says: *"Those who obey his commands live in him, and he in them. And this is how we know that he lives in us: We know it by the Spirit he gave us."* In 1 John 4:13-15 we read,

> *We know we live in him and he in us, because he has given us of his Spirit. And we have seen and do testify that the Father has sent his Son to be the Savior of the world. If anyone acknowledges that Jesus is the Son of God, God lives in him and he in God."*

Paul, the apostle says that no one can confess that Jesus is Lord except by the Holy Spirit of God.[14] Paul also says in Romans 8:16: *"The Spirit himself testifies with our spirit that we are God's children."* How does the Holy Spirit do that? He speaks to us inwardly giving us understanding of spiritual things. There is a peace that the Holy Spirit gives that we are right with God.

It is one of the tasks of the Holy Spirit of God to give you understanding of God's Word. The apostle Paul writes in 1 Corinthians 2:12, *"We have not received the spirit of the world but the Spirit who is from God, that we may understand what God has freely given us."* In verse 14 he also says, *"The man without the Spirit does not accept the things that come from the Spirit of God, for they are foolishness to him, and he cannot understand them, because they are spiritually discerned."*

Do you find the gospel about Jesus Christ and His shed blood on the cross in payment for your sins to be a precious truth that you now treasure? Or is it still foolishness to you? If it is treasured as wonderful and precious, it is because Christ Jesus has given you the Holy Spirit in your life. As you read the Bible now, do you find things beginning to make sense to you which you never understood before? It is because of the witness and teaching of the Holy Spirit in your heart and mind.

- **Do you accept and submit to the truth that is found in God's written Word?**

---

[14] 1 Corinthians 12:3

Christians submit to the authority of God and therefore accept what God says as His truth. Those who truly have Jesus Christ living in their lives desire to live under the Lordship of Jesus Christ. 1 John 4:6 says, *"We are from God, and whoever knows God listens to us; but whoever is not from God does not listen to us. This is how we recognize the Spirit of truth and the spirit of error."* John was one of the apostles commissioned by God and inspired of God to complete God's written word. As such, the apostles were writing the truth of God which has the authority of the Sovereign God. The true Christian accepts what was given through the apostles as God's truth that has authority in his life. It is by the authority of this same Word of God that you can know that you have eternal life (1 John 5:13).

Have you come to the point where you accept the Bible as being God's revealed Word and that the Bible is your authority for your life? Does the Word of God speak to you when you read it? Does it bring conviction in your life when something that does not please God is still a part of your life? This is strong evidence that Jesus Christ has come into your life and you are born again.

- **Are you experiencing the love of God in your heart?**

1 John 4:7-12 says,

> *Dear friends, let us love one another, for love comes from God. Everyone who loves has been born of God and knows God. Whoever does not love does not know God, because God is love. This is how God showed his love among us: He sent his one and only Son as an atoning sacrifice for our sins. Dear friends, since God so loved us, we also ought to love one another. No one has ever seen God; but if we love one another, God lives in us and his love is made complete in us.*

Do you find yourself overwhelmed at times by God's great love? By the fact that He sent His only Son to the cross for you? It was a great sacrifice for both the Father and the Son? Do you find that you want to share that same love by giving yourself to others to meet their needs? Do you find more compassion toward others growing in your heart? That is God's love in your life and it is another sign that Christ Jesus lives in you.

Distinguish between babyhood and maturity

You might be saying to yourself right now, "I see some fruit but not very much! I see some evidence that Christ is in my life, but there is so much that is still not like Christ!" That is true of all of us.

Do not make the mistake of thinking that you are not saved because you find yourself still failing Christ or you find that your love for others is not always as it should be. Realize that you are a baby Christian and you need to grow up to be a mature Christian. That takes time. In fact, you will never be completely mature and completely like Christ until you are home in heaven.

I planted a new peach tree in our garden recently. I got it from the nursery as a tree that has about three or four years of growth. I will be pleasantly surprised if it bears a few peaches this season along with leaves. But each year, with proper care by me, the gardener, it will become more and more fruitful. In John 15, Jesus said that the Father is the gardener and he will care for you and prune you so that you will produce more fruit. As you continue to abide or remain in Christ Jesus, the vine, the time will come when you will produce much fruit.

It will last forever

So, did you pass the tests? Yes, there is some fruit. Yes, there is some evidence that Jesus Christ has indeed made you alive spiritually. Then rest your mind and heart in the fact that you are saved from your sin and you have the gift of eternal life. It will last forever.

Christ Jesus always keeps His promises. When we meet His conditions of repentance and faith, then He keeps His word. He indeed comes to live in us and raises us to new life in Him. We have confidence also that we are going to be with the Lord in heaven because we are kept by God's power, not our own. John 10:27-30 has a powerful promise for you as a believer in Christ.

> *My sheep listen to my voice; I know them and they follow me. I give them eternal life, and they shall never perish; no one can snatch them out of my hand. My Father, who has given them to me, is greater than all; no one can snatch them out of my Father's hand. I and the Father are one.*

All State Insurance Company advertised that "you are in good hands with All State!" When God redeems you from your sin and gives you eternal life, you are in His protective hands. You are in good hands when you are in the heavenly Father's hands! When you are known by the great Shepherd, Jesus Christ, as one of His flock, you can never be lost from Him ever again. He will keep you safe and guide you home to heaven.

The apostle Paul shared a great promise with the believers in Rome in Romans 8:38-39:

> *For I am convinced that neither death nor life, neither angels nor demons, neither the present nor the future, nor any powers, neither height nor depth, nor anything else in all creation, will be able to separate us from the love of God that is in Christ Jesus.*

Some study questions for your reflection

1. What evidence do I see that I have been born again and that Jesus Christ now lives in me?
2. How does the fruit of the Spirit come about in my life?
3. How do I remain a Christian? Is it by my effort or God's work?
4. According to John 10:27-30, how can I be sure that I will have eternal life in heaven?
5. Am I arrogant or bragging if I say "I know I am going to heaven?"
6. How can I be sure that I will go to heaven?
7. What if I do not see as much love for other people as I would like to see? Does that mean I am not saved? What does it mean?
8. How can I become more fruitful as a follower of Jesus Christ?
9. How can I be sure that I will never be separated from God again?

Chapter Three

When I Sin, What Do I Do?

A reality check

So you've gone through the tests. You know that you are truly born again and that you are saved for eternity. While there is evidence that Jesus Christ has entered your life and you are changed by His power, yet you are aware that you still do things that are wrong. You find that you think wrong thoughts at times and your attitude is not always like Christ, your new-found Savior and Lord. Your words do not always please God and your actions from time to time are not right. In other words, you still sin.

Some Christians feel that they have come to the point that they never sin anymore. Even the fact that they believe that they are now perfect is in itself sin, because such a belief is pride and arrogance before God. They need to take a reality check! Kick such a person in the shins and see if he is sinless in his reaction. Talk to his wife. Quiz her husband. Ask their children if they think their parents never sin anymore. The reality is that all Christians still sin. In fact, the more we grow in our knowledge of the Bible and the closer we walk with God, the more acutely aware we will be of the sins in our lives. We will begin to see attitudes, thoughts, words and actions as sinful that we previously thought were alright.

So what does the fact that I still commit some sins mean? Does it mean that I'm not really a Christian? No, if the whole pattern of your life is not total darkness, you are a Christian who walks in the light of Jesus Christ. However, from time to time, you still do that which displeases your Lord and Savior. Does the fact that you still sin mean that you lose your gift of eternal life? No, God the Father has you in His good hands and He will keep you as His own forever. He does not disown you as His child when you fall into sin.

To be in right relationship with God in your life today does not require that you live perfectly or without sin. It means that you must not allow your sin to go unchecked or unconfessed. You must do what God tells you to do about your sin. So let's see what God shows us about sin in the Christian's life.

God does not want you to sin

1 John 2:1-2 is a very important passage in the Bible.

> *My dear children, I write this to you so that you will not sin. But if anybody does sin, we have one who speaks to the Father in our defense - Jesus Christ, the Righteous One. He is the atoning sacrifice for our sins, and not only for ours but also for the sins of the whole world.*

It is never God's will for us to sin, so never make an excuse for your sinning or blame God for your sinning. Notice John's words: *"I write this to you so that you will not sin."* Satan will want you to rationalize your sin, making allowance for your sinful behavior with all kinds of excuses. "I couldn't help it!" or "It wasn't my fault!" Like Adam and Eve in the garden, they both blamed someone else for their failure. Adam said, in essence, "It is this woman you gave me, God. If you hadn't given me this woman, then I would not have sinned." In finality, he was blaming God Himself for making the mistake of giving him Eve as his wife. Eve blamed Satan. Rather than blaming herself, she blamed Satan.[15] What sounded reasonable was really just an excuse for making her wrong choice.

Your attitude as a follower of Jesus Christ should be that you never want to sin against God. In other words, your attitude should always be to walk obediently and to live in a way that brings praise and glory to Jesus Christ.

God recognizes you will sin

Immediately after telling us that God doesn't want us to sin, John makes it clear that we will sin. John promptly says, *"But, if anybody does sin . . ."* In 1 John 1:8, John has already said to us as Christians: *"If we claim to be without sin, we deceive ourselves and the truth is not in us."*

---

[15] Genesis 3:8-13

So, don't deny that you sin. Rather, always be sensitive to the Holy Spirit convicting you of sin. The Holy Spirit will speak to you in your conscience, guiding you according to the Word of God. When you are sinning, He will make you aware of it. God then expects you to respond to the Holy Spirit's convicting voice by repenting from your sin. The apostle Paul wrote in Ephesians 4:30 *"And do not grieve the Holy Spirit of God, with whom you were sealed for the day of redemption."* We grieve God's Spirit when we sin but we grieve Him even more by resisting Him when He shows us our sin. It is only as the Holy Spirit makes you aware of your sin that you can deal with sin. The Holy Spirit will primarily show you your sin as you are studying the Word of God, the Bible.

A contrast from Scripture

Two of the disciples of Jesus stand in great contrast when it comes to the matter of sin and their response to their denial of Christ Jesus.

We see Judas, on the one hand, who was chosen by Christ to be one of His twelve followers. Judas revealed the unsaved nature of his heart by intentionally conspiring with the high priest to betray Jesus into the hands of His enemies. For thirty pieces of silver, he sold Jesus to be tried and crucified by His captors. When he sought to give back the money, the chief priests refused it. His unrepentant heart is disclosed by his actions. Instead of coming to God and repenting from his sin, he went out and hung himself.

On the other hand, we see the disciple, Peter, also called by Christ to be one of his twelve disciples. On the night of Jesus' trial, Peter is found cowering in the outer courtyard. Just as Jesus predicted, Peter denied that he even knew Jesus. When confronted by mere servant girls, he denied Jesus three times, even with oaths and cursing. The rooster crowed and Peter is smitten in his heart that the prophecy of Jesus was true. Matthew 26:34 records the words of Jesus to Peter: *"I tell you the truth," Jesus answered, "this very night, before the rooster crows, you will disown me three times."* Peter's reaction to his sin is totally different from that of Judas. Matthew 26:75 shows Peter's sorrow and repentance. *"Then Peter remembered the words Jesus had spoken: 'Before the rooster crows, you will disown me three times.' And he went outside and wept bitterly."*

The non-Christian may feel some remorse over some gross sin; he may even sense some temporary sorrow for what he has done. His sorrow does not lead to repentance and confession of his sin. While the true Christian on the other hand may resist the Holy Spirit's conviction for a time, ultimately he will repent with deep heart-felt sorrow. Paul speaks of godly sorrow and worldly sorrow as he writes in 2 Corinthians 7:10: *"Godly sorrow brings repentance that leads to salvation and leaves no regret, but worldly sorrow brings death."* One of the signs that Christ Jesus has truly changed your heart is how you feel about your sin and how you deal with it. Do you see your sin as a great offense to God? Does your sin cause you great pain in your heart? Are you truly repentant in your heart and are you willing to confess your sin?

When you sin, this is what God expects

1 John 1:9 is written to and for true Christians. *"If we confess our sins, he is faithful and just and will forgive us our sins and purify us from all unrighteousness."* This verse is not written to unbelievers and is not intended to tell the sinner how to be born again. Sinners are not born again by simply asking Christ to forgive their sins. The issue is repenting from their sin and trusting Jesus Christ as Savior and Lord. It is not simply a matter of a sinner listing off some specific sins and seeking God's forgiveness. He must deal with the deeper issue of his sinful life because he has been going his own independent way and living his own sinful life. Will he repent from that rebelliousness and let Jesus Christ come into his life to cleanse him, or will he remain in the deadness of his sin?

This verse is God's instruction to the Christian about what he is to do when he sins. He is to confess his sin. The word "confess" could be literally translated "to say the same thing." It means that you agree with God that what you have done is sin just as God has said. Confessing your sin is coming to the point of acknowledging that God is right in judging your act as sin.

You cease making excuses for your action and accept God's judgment instead. So, as a Christian, you are to deal with specific sins, as the Lord convicts you of them. Name your sin specifically and agree with God that you have sinned in this particular way.

Confession involves abandoning your sin. You cannot confess your sin and continue on sinning as if God does not care about what you have done. There is a repentant attitude in your heart by which you decide that you no longer want to continue in your sinful way.

When you confess your sin to the Lord, are you then willing to believe God's promise to you? He says that if you confess your sin, he is willing to forgive your sin and to purify you from your sin. The word that the New International Version translates as "purify" is from a word that means to "cleanse" or to "clean up." As a Christian, when you sin, you need not only to be forgiven for your sin; you also need to be cleaned up again. To "forgive" means that God sends your sin and its penalty away from you. To "cleanse" means that God also cleans you from sin's stains so that you can again walk in a pure way before Him.

When our son was just three years of age, his mother bathed him and got him all dressed up in clean clothes in preparation to go to church. She told him not to go outside so that he would not get dirty. As she was getting herself dressed for church, our son was disobedient - he sinned against his mother. He went outside and got into some mud. When his mother saw him, she reprimanded him. Our son was immediately sorry for his action and pleaded with his mother to forgive him. Of course, he received her forgiveness. However, he needed to be cleaned up again and to be dressed in clean clothes to completely remove the result of his sinful action.

So it is for you as a Christian. God not only forgives you for your sin; He cleanses you from your sin so that you will enjoy His righteousness again in your Christian walk. Then you must trust God's promise to you. Satan is an accuser and will seek to accuse you about your sin even after you have confessed your sin to the Lord. Refuse his accusations and instead believe what God says in His Word. Don't continue to walk in guilt and don't continue to chastise yourself because you have sinned. Thank the Lord for His forgiveness and cleansing and move forward in the freedom and in joy of the Lord.

Repeated sins and enslaving habits

No one can sin without consequences. The Christian may suffer some results of his sin even though God forgives him and cleanses him. This is another reason why the Christian should always seek for victory over temptation that he may not sin against God. It is better to avoid falling into temptation and sinning against God in the first place. It is better to avoid an accident with your car than to fix the damage after an accident.

A Christian father was trying to teach his son about sin and its effects. When his son would do some wrong thing, he would pound a nail into the kitchen door. As his son would come and ask for forgiveness, he would allow his son to pull out the nail. One day his son said to his father, "Dad, I have pulled out the nails, but there are still holes in the door." His father told him that God will forgive him when he confesses his sin but there are always scars that remain from sin.

Before you have been a Christian for very long, you will realize that you are confessing a sin that you have confessed before, perhaps several times. Satan will try to convince you that God won't forgive you again for a repeated sin. That is Satan's lie! However the Lord Jesus desires that we find victory over temptation which he provides rather than having to come and seek His forgiveness over and over again. Jesus' words, as recorded in John 8:34-36, offer us His freedom.

> *Jesus replied, "I tell you the truth, everyone who sins is a slave to sin. Now a slave has no permanent place in the family, but a son belongs to it forever. So if the Son sets you free, you will be free indeed."*

As a true believer in Jesus Christ, you have Christ living in you and you have God's Holy Spirit dwelling in you. Therefore, as a born again Christian, you have Christ's power in your life to resist temptation and you have His victory to keep you from falling.

Throw off hindering and entangling things

The author of Hebrews writes in Hebrews 12:1-2:

> *Therefore, since we are surrounded by such a great cloud of witnesses,[16] let us throw off everything that hinders and the sin that so easily entangles us, and let us run with perseverance the race marked out for us. Let us fix our eyes on Jesus, the author and perfecter of our faith, who for the joy set before him endured the cross, scorning its shame, and sat down at the right hand of the throne of God.*

There are some things that hinder us from running the Christian race just like there are some things that hinder a runner competing in the Olympics. A runner could run with heavy boots on his feet or a heavy winter coat on his body, but this would not be wise. If he is going to run a good race, he will throw off everything that will hinder him from running well. So it is with us as Christians. There are some things that may not be in themselves sinful, but if they hinder us from being our best for Jesus, then we are exhorted to throw them off. For example, there is nothing specifically sinful about a television set. However, if we are watching evil stuff on the set that is filling our minds with evil thoughts, we are to quit watching the television because it is getting in the way of having a pure mind before the Lord. Or if we are watching something that is perfectly good on television, but it is taking up our time that we ought to be using in studying God's Word, then we need to shut off the television that is hindering us from doing something more worthwhile. If we want to run the Christian race well, we must discipline ourselves to throw off anything that hinders us from running our best race for Christ.

The writer also mentions *"the sin that so easily entangles us."* The sin that easily entangles one Christian may be entirely different from the sin that entangles another Christian. For example, I personally was raised in a Christian home where my father taught me to avoid alcoholic beverages. He taught me that it was the wise way to live. He said, "If you set your mind to live your life without partaking of alcoholic drinks, you will never have the problem of becoming addicted to alcohol." So, for me, alcohol is not a sin that easily entangles me. I'm never tempted to take

---

16 The "cloud of witnesses "is found in the previous chapter, Hebrews 11, where a whole list of believers are mentioned who have already run the race and been faithful to God. They are already in heaven.

even one drink. However, for another Christian, who has had a problem with alcohol, this is a great temptation. Raised in a different atmosphere, having learned to drink alcohol with his friends, he may find the temptation to drink alcohol, and ultimately getting drunk, is a sin that easily entangles him. He should throw it off! In fact, he shouldn't allow himself to get into situations where he will be tempted.

The temptation that can lead me to a sin that easily entangles me is good food in abundance. Eating is not the sin but over-eating is. It leads to my gaining weight beyond that which is good for me. So I make it a practice to avoid going to "all you can eat" buffets. I must throw off the sin that so easily entangles me.

Enslaving habits

Enslaving habits come from allowing Satan to have a foothold in our lives rather than allowing Jesus Christ to be in control of our lives. Have you surrendered your entire life to the Lord Jesus? Or are you keeping some areas under your own control?

God has given us certain basic drives in our lives. Enslaving habits entangle us because of wrongfully satisfying legitimate physical and emotional drives given to us by God.

There is the normal drive to eat when we experience the sense of hunger. It is necessary and good for our survival. When eating food to survive becomes an obsession for food, whether hungry or not, it becomes an enslaving habit. Another normal drive is to drink in order not to become dehydrated; the intake of liquids is necessary for our survival. However, if my thirst leads to drinking those things that enslave me and produce drunkenness, then it becomes an enslaving habit.

The sex drive is a legitimate drive. God has given us hormones that kick in as we mature physically for the continual propagation of the human race. The sex drive is also for pleasure but it is confined by God to the marriage relationship. When this God-given drive is allowed to be satisfied in evil ways, it is an enslaving habit that becomes destructive and is sinful. Many enslaving habits result from this basic powerful legitimate human drive.

Are there sins that are enslaving you? Are you addicted to food? Are you a slave to drugs or alcoholic beverages? Are you trapped into premarital or extramarital sexual relationships? Are you indulging yourself in deceptive and destructive evils such as pornography and other twisted sinful behaviors that come from Satan himself?

"I want to be free," you say. "How can I gain victory over my enslaving habit?" Paul, the apostle, gives us some insights in Romans 6:6, 11-14.[17]

> *For we know that our old self was crucified with him so that the body of sin might be done away with, that we should no longer be slaves to sin. . . . In the same way, count yourselves dead to sin but alive to God in Christ Jesus. Therefore do not let sin reign in your mortal body so that you obey its evil desires. Do not offer the parts of your body so that you obey its evil desires. Do not offer the parts of your body to sin, as instruments of wickedness, but rather offer yourselves to God, as those who have been brought from death to life; and offer the parts of your body to him as instruments of righteousness. For sin shall not be your master, because you are not under law but under grace.*

Paul gives four steps to gain victory over the slavery of sin.

- Know this fact that when Christ died on the cross, your old sinful flesh (sinful nature) was put to death there on the cross. So Jesus Christ already makes the provision for your freedom from your enslaving sinful habit on the cross (Verse 6). It is very important to know what Christ has already done for you. Don't struggle by your own strength. Believe what Christ has done for you. Trust in the fact that Christ Jesus has already defeated Satan and sin on the cross. Your victory is guaranteed by Christ's victory!
- Count this fact to be true in your life (Verse 11). Unless you recognize that the provision is made in Christ and unless you now consider this fact to be true for you personally, you will never gain victory. So claim what

---

[17] It will be a good exercise for you to read the entire chapter of Romans 6.

Christ has done for you for your own personal experience today.
- Refuse to allow sin to be your master (Verse 12). Refuse to let Satan be in charge of your life and refuse to let sin win the victory over you. Refuse to be permanently defeated. As Winston Churchill once said, when Britain was facing defeat in World War II, "Never, never, never, never give up!" So each time you fall into this enslaving behavior, don't give up. Confess your sin, accept the Lord's forgiveness and cleansing and trust Christ to deliver you.
- Offer your body and the parts of your body as tools for doing what is right, not what is wrong (Verses 13-14). What you continually give your body to do, will be your master. So continually offer your body as a living sacrifice to God. See also Romans 12:1-2. Victory is found as you allow Christ to be Lord and Master every moment of every day, yielding your body to Him to live in ways that please and honor Him.

Another very helpful passage of Scripture is 1 Corinthians 10:12-13.

> *So if you think you are standing firm, be careful that you don't fall! No temptation has seized you except what is common to man. And God is faithful; he will not let you be tempted beyond what you can bear. But when you are tempted, he will also provide a way out so that you can stand up under it.*

In the previous verses Paul writes about the experiences of the nation of Israel as they wandered in the wilderness before entering into Canaan land that had been promised to them. He writes about Israel's sins and their disobedience toward God. He tells us that all these things have been recorded for our benefit that we would not make the same mistakes and sin in the same ways that Israel did. I will just highlight some truths from these verses that have helped me gain victory over some enslaving habits in my life.

- Don't become overconfident and think that you now have it under control, just because you haven't fallen for a while (Verse 12). The minute you think you have the enslaving habit under control, you are vulnerable to fall. Our

confidence must continually be in Christ Jesus, our Savior and Lord, and not in ourselves.
- Don't excuse your sin by saying that you have it worse than others or no one knows how powerful your temptation is. The temptation that you are going through is the same as others experience; it is common to all people.
- When you fall into sin, it is not God's failure to provide for you. God is always faithful to you. He has promised that He is with you always and will never leave you or forsake you. So do not be guilty of blaming God by saying "God, you made me this way. That is why I sin."
- God will never allow your temptation to be greater than what He knows you are able to stand. So with Christ living in you and with the Holy Spirit's power available to you, you do have the power to overcome your temptation.
- God always provides a way out of your temptation. Through Christ's death on the cross, through prayer, through God's Word, and through the Holy Spirit empowering your life, you do have a way out. In other words, there is no excuse for your sin.
- So accept responsibility for your habit and for your failure to gain victory. When you make excuses, you are playing into Satan's deceptions. Excuses will never provide you with victory over your enslaving sinful habits. Christ Jesus will!

An example for your encouragement

All sin is horrible in God's sight. However, some sins are more public and more devastating in the damage they do to us and to others. There are some sins for which we have a hard time accepting God's forgiveness because to us they seem more hideous than other sins.

Sometimes we deal with our sin in God's prescribed ways. We have forsaken our sin, confessed it to the Lord and sought to accept God's forgiveness and cleansing. However, we can't seem to rest in God's forgiveness. Satan keeps accusing and causing us to think that God won't forgive hideous sin. He wants us to believe that God can and will forgive some lesser sins, but not "this one" that we have committed.

Let's consider King David as our example.[18] If God would forgive him, will he not forgive you? King David was a man after God's own heart and he followed the Lord almost all of his life. However King David grew careless in guarding his life and ended up committing some hideous sins that caused great damage to him, to others and to God. His sins brought reproach upon God's name and had long-term negative results in his reign as king of Israel.

King David was walking on his palace roof at night when he couldn't sleep. He observed a beautiful woman, Bathsheba, taking a bath. So he kept watching and allowed lust to build in his mind and heart. He allowed the wrong desires to lead him to send for her, probably justifying his actions by reminding himself that he was the king. He slept with her and she became pregnant. Then David tried to cover his sin by calling her husband home from the battle field, to hopefully make it appear that it was not his child, but her husband's child. But Uriah would not cooperate and refused to sleep with his wife while his comrades were out at war. So David committed another sin by ordering the army's retreat, leaving Uriah vulnerable to be killed. So David is also guilty of murder. Then he took Bathsheba as his wife.

David covered over his sin and refused to admit that he had sinned until the prophet, Nathan, came to him with God's convicting message. Only then did David deal with his sin.

Psalm 51 is David's account of honestly coming clean before God and dealing with his hideous sins. He confessed his sin and sought for God's cleansing from his sin. He then came to accept God's forgiveness and was restored to serving the Lord again. In fact, God inspired David to write Psalm 32:1-5.

> *Blessed is he whose transgressions are forgiven, whose sins are covered. Blessed is the man whose sin the LORD does not count against him and in whose spirit is no deceit. When I kept silent, my bones wasted away through my groaning all day long. For day and night your hand was heavy upon me; my strength was sapped as in the heat of summer. Then*

---

[18] You may read this account in 2 Samuel 11, 12.

> *I acknowledged my sin to you and did not cover up my iniquity. I said, "I will confess my transgressions to the LORD," and you will forgive the guilt of my sin."*

The Psalmist David shares the truth about his sin and the blessing of God's forgiveness. Contemplate David's words and apply them to your own life. Deal with your sin honestly and completely before God. Then rest in his forgiveness and cleansing.

Some study questions for your reflection

1. Have you discovered that you still find yourself sinning even though you know you are a born again Christian? What are some of the ways you have discovered that you still sin?
2. What does your sin mean? Does it mean that you are no longer a Christian? Does it mean that God disowns you as His child because you have sinned?
3. As a Christian, what should your attitude be toward sin? Should a Christian ever intentionally want to sin?
4. The reality is that you will find that you do sin. What does God ask you to do about your sin?
5. What does God promise He will do for you if you honestly confess your sin to Him?
6. Do you find yourself struggling with some habit that you know is not pleasing to God?
7. What are God's instructions to you that will enable you to gain victory over your enslaving habit?
8. What do we learn about ourselves from King David's experiences as he was entrapped in his sins? Is there some lesson about avoiding the traps of sin? When we do sin, what lessons do we learn from David about dealing with our sin?

Chapter Four

The Word Of God In Your Life!

The Bible is a unique book! There is no other book like it. Why? The Bible is the Word of God. This means that the Bible is God's special revelation to man in written form. The Word of God came by inspiration of the Holy Spirit writing through human writers. The apostle Peter says in 2 Peter 1:20-21, "... *no prophecy of Scripture is of any private interpretation, for prophecy never came by the will of man, but holy men of God spoke as they were moved by the Holy Spirit."*

God's revealed Scripture was completed through chosen *holy men* and no other revelation is needed. The apostle Peter says in 2 Peter 1:3,

> *His divine power has given to us all things that pertain to life and godliness, through the knowledge of Him who called us by glory and virtue, by which have been given to us exceedingly great and precious promises, that through these you may be partakers of the divine nature, having escaped the corruption that is in the world through lust.*

God has given us all that we need to know God and to find eternal life through His Son, Jesus Christ.

God has revealed Himself through all that He has created, so that we can know of His existence and His power.[19] As we look around us and meditate on the created universe, the logical conclusion is that there is a Great Intelligent Cause of all that we see. As we contemplate the intricacy of His creative care in the details of nature, we may conclude that God cares for us in providing for us to live on this earth. However, we can never know of God's love for us and of His prepared way to heaven without God speaking to us in the Bible. God has revealed to us that He loves us and that He has provided His Son, Jesus Christ, as the means of saving us from our sin. That is why we treasure

---

[19] Romans 1:20 says "For since the creation of the world His invisible attributes are clearly seen, being understood by the things that are made, even His eternal power and Godhead, so that they are without excuse . . ."

the Bible and desire to grow to know our Great God better through the study of His revealed Word.

God provides the food

Just as we need to eat regularly in order to nurture our bodies physically, so we also are in need of daily spiritual nourishment in order to maintain a vital relationship with God. When God delivered Israel from slavery in Egypt by His miraculous works, they were taken into the wilderness area where they were faced with starvation. They complained against God, believing that God had delivered them through the Exodus from Egypt only that they might die in the desert. God provided daily food for them called manna. It was a light bread-like substance that came each morning as the dew dried up. The people had to gather the manna for themselves daily.[20]

In John 6 we read the account of Jesus feeding the five thousand by multiplying five barley loaves and two small fish. As the people flocked to Jesus on the next day, Jesus told them that He was the bread of life that came down from heaven. In verses 48-51 Jesus said,

> *I am the bread of life. Your fathers ate the manna in the wilderness, and are dead. This is the bread which comes down from heaven, that one may eat of it and not die. I am the living bread which came down from heaven. If anyone eats of this bread, he will live forever; and the bread that I shall give is My flesh, which I shall give for the life of the world.*

The Word of God is given to us by the Father to reveal Jesus Christ to us as the living Word of God. Your soul will be refreshed and your life will be nourished spiritually as you study God's holy Word, the Bible. Let God speak to you through His Word.

The apostle Peter wrote in 1 Peter 2:2:

> *Therefore, laying aside all malice, all deceit, hypocrisy, envy, and all evil speaking, as newborn babes, desire the*

---

[20] Read Exodus 16 for an account of the giving of the manna.

> *pure milk of the word, that you may grow thereby, if indeed you have tasted that the Lord is gracious.*

As a new Christian, you need to ingest the milk of the Word of God so that you will grow into maturity as a Christian.

The writer of Hebrews speaks about the solid food of the Word that is meant for maturing Christians. In Hebrews 5:12-14, he chastises his readers because they had not been growing up to be mature Christians. He says,

> *For though by this time you ought to be teachers, you need someone to teach you again the first principles of the oracles of God; and you have come to need milk and not solid food. For everyone who partakes only of milk is unskilled in the word of righteousness, for he is a babe. But solid food belongs to those who are of full age, that is, those who by reason of use have their senses exercised to discern both good and evil.*

The milk of the Word is the important basic truths about Christ and your relationship with God that is the necessary foundation for Christian growth. The Word of God contains many deep truths that are the solid food of the Word of God. For example, the nature of our God is very complex and He is beyond the level of our full comprehension. As you seek to grow in your understanding of God and His marvelous ways, you will find you are grappling with digesting of the solid food of God's Word.

It is important for you, as a new Christian, to focus on the basic truths that will delight your soul. As you grow in Christ, you will discover more and more about Christ - how He loves and provides for you. Don't get concerned about the heavier teachings that you are not yet equipped to understand as a new baby in God's redeemed family. Remember, babies do not start out on solid food immediately after birth.

A daily time for God's Word

Just as Israel needed to gather manna every day, it is important for you to set aside a special time to read and study God's Word. Christians often refer to this time as "my devotions" or "my quiet time with the Lord." It is a time when you allow God to speak to you through His Word.

I suggest that you establish a time as you arise in the morning. D. L. Moody used to say to his students, "No Bible, no breakfast." This is the time when you are rested and it is always important to begin your busy day by focusing your attention upon Jesus Christ, your Savior and your Lord. Begin your day by making certain that you have no unconfessed sin in your life. Do you want to walk in obedience to Jesus today? Do you want God's will to be done in your life today? Then seek to know Him better by spending a few minutes in His Word. Let Him speak to you through His Word.

Some people are 'night' people and the morning is not the best time for them. Their metabolism does not allow them to awaken quickly to a new day. For them, some other time of the day may be better. The important thing is not when you find your "quiet time" with the Lord Jesus. Do not neglect this important appointment in your day. Plan a specific time and discipline yourself to read the Word of God. It will be an invaluable investment of your time and energy.

Satan will do his best to keep you from the Word of God. He will seek to distract you in every way possible. He will seek to tell you that you are too busy to take the time to read God's Word. He knows that the Christian who neglects the Word of God doesn't stand a chance of being a strong vital Christian. Someone has said: "Seven days without the Word of God makes one weak!"

Some practical suggestions

- Splash some cold water in your face and refresh yourself in the morning before you sit down to read your Bible. Especially if you are not a "morning person," your body will benefit from a wake-up call.

- Begin your systematic reading of the Bible in the New Testament. A good book to begin with is the Gospel of John, followed by the Epistle of First John. If you are unfamiliar with the Bible, there is a table of contents in the front of each Bible, listing the books of the Bible and the pages on which you will find them.

- If you do not have a modern translation of the Bible, you will want to get a good Bible to read. Go to any Christian bookstore and you will find an abundance of translations. I would recommend the New King James Version, the New International Version, or the New American Standard Version for serious Bible study. The Living Bible Translation completed in 1996 is a very reliable paraphrase that is refreshing in its simplicity and style. Be aware that some cult groups such as the Jehovah's Witnesses and the Mormons have their own translations that are altered in various places to support some of their false teachings.

- Make use of a good devotional guide. Be certain that you look up the assigned passage from the Bible and read it. After all, it is God's Word that you need more than the commentary of other Christians, as good and profitable as their comments may be. Here are a couple of suggestions for daily devotional guides.[21]

- Applying the truth of the Bible to your life is absolutely essential to grow in your new relationship with God. Jesus commissioned his disciples to make other disciples (followers), to baptize those new disciples and then to continue to teach them to obey all the things, which he taught them.[22] Notice that it is not enough to simply mentally know what Jesus taught us but to obey or do the things that He taught. James 1:22-25 says,

> *But be doers of the Word, and not hearers only, deceiving yourselves. For if anyone is a hearer of the word and not a doer, he is like a man observing his natural face in a mirror; for he observes himself, goes away, and immediately forgets what kind of man he was. But he who looks into the perfect law of liberty and continues in it, and is not a forgetful hearer but a doer of the work, this one will be blessed in what he does.*

---

[21] Our Daily Bread, printed and distributed by RBC Ministries, PO Box 2222, Grand Rapids, MI 49501-2222. By writing your request for Our Daily Bread, you can receive it free every month. Another good guide for the more mature Christian is Today In The Word, published and distributed by Moody Bible Institute, Chicago, IL. You may request your free monthly copy by writing Today In the Word, 820 N. LaSalle Blvd., Chicago, IL 60610

[22] Matthew 28:18-20.

I suggest that you get a notebook in which you can make brief notes of the thoughts that come to you as you read the Bible. Make notations and pray these thoughts into your life. Taking time to review these notes from time to time can be an encouraging time in your life. Asking questions of the portion of the Bible you are reading will help you to apply the truth of the Bible to your life. Questions such as these will make the Bible come alive for you.

1. Does this passage of Scripture show me any new truth or emphasize some truth I already know about God that will enable me to know and worship Him today?

2. Does this passage convict me of any sin or show me any failure that I need to correct in my life today?

3. Is God speaking to me about anything that I need to do for Him today?

4. Is there some promise from God in the Scripture passage that I need to claim as I seek to grow in my faith in Christ today?

5. Is there some unanswered question to which I need to seek the answer from a more mature Christian?

• Memorize special Bible verses that speak to you personally. Hiding God's Word in your heart will enable your mind to recall those verses in times of special need or when you are seeking to share the gospel with a non Christian. Write out the verse you want to memorize on a card that you can carry with you. When you have a few spare minutes during your day, review the verses. Your effort to memorize Scripture will pay great dividends as you permanently tuck these verses away in your mind and heart.

The Bible: every Christian's authority

The Bible is the Word of God. The Bible is God's truth revealed without error through the work of God's Holy Spirit through human writers. Therefore the Bible is God's authority in the Christian's life.

There will be many times when you will come upon passages of Scripture that you find difficult to understand. Or you may think there are contradictions in the Bible. The Bible has been vindicated many, many times as its enemies have pointed out what they believe to be 'errors'. Archaeologists have made many discoveries that have proven some disputed fact of history to be true or have authenticated the claims of the Bible in various other ways. Through research in the Scriptures, you will find that apparent contradictions melt away and the Bible proves to be true and trustworthy. The apostle Peter affirms the trustworthiness of the Word of God in 1 Peter 1:23,25: " . . . *having been born again, not of corruptible seed but incorruptible, through the Word of God which lives and abides forever*" . . . "*But the Word of the LORD endures forever.*"

Jesus affirmed the authority of the Bible as God's Word. In Matthew 5:17-18, Jesus says,

> *Do not think that I came to destroy the Law or the Prophets. I did not come to destroy but to fulfill. For assuredly, I say to you, till heaven and earth pass away, one jot or one tittle [23] will by no means pass from the law till all is fulfilled.*

Some benefits gained from God's Word

Psalm 119 is a lengthy psalm of 176 verses, almost every one of which refers in some way to the Word of God. Consider a few of the benefits that come from consistently studying the Word of God.

• You will be blessed as you read and obey His Word. Psalm 119:1-2 says, "*Blessed are the undefiled in the way, Who walk in the law of the LORD! Blessed are those who keep His testimonies, Who seek Him with the whole heart!*"

• You will keep your heart right and your life clean before God. Psalm 119:9-11 reads: "*How can a young man cleanse his way? By taking heed according to Your Word. With my whole heart I have sought You; Oh, let me not wander from Your*

---

[23] "one jot or one tittle" - A "jot" refers to the smallest Hebrew letter, the yohd , which is a meager stroke of the pen, like an accent mark or an apostrophe. The "tittle" is a tiny extension on a Hebrew letter, like the serif in modern typefaces. From The McArthur Study Bible, Word Bibles, 1997, p. 1400.

commandments! Your Word I have hidden in my heart, That I might not sin against You."

- You will be revived when you are struggling with your emotions and you will be strengthened in your inner being. Psalm 119:25, 28 speak of this benefit from being in the Word of God. *"My soul clings to the dust; Revive me according to Your word . . . My soul melts from heaviness; Strengthen me according to Your word."*

- Your heart will be glad, giving you a rejoicing spirit even in the night time hours. Psalm 119:54, 62 tell us *"Your statutes have been my songs in the house of my pilgrimage . . . At midnight I will rise to give thanks to You, Because of Your righteous judgments."*

- Your confidence in God is renewed and settled as you read the Word of God and believe it. In times of doubt, you are reassured that God is Sovereign and His promises are true and dependable. Psalm 119:89-90 says *"Forever, O LORD, Your word is settled in heaven. Your faithfulness endures to all generations; You established the earth, and it abides."*

- You will become wise as you study and believe God's Word. Your wisdom comes from Him as the Holy Spirit guides you into His truth. Psalm 119:98-100 speaks of this wisdom received through constant meditation upon the word of God.

> *You, through Your commandments, make me wiser than my enemies; For they are ever with me. I have more understanding than all my teachers, For Your testimonies are my meditation. I understand more than the ancients, Because I keep Your precepts.*

Do not become conceited or arrogant, thinking that you now know all things and do not need to listen to good Christian teachers. The Psalmist is speaking about wisdom that comes from God's Word that non-Christian teachers fail to see because they do not know and accept God's truth. The prophet, Isaiah, clearly teaches us that God's thoughts are far above man's thoughts and His ways far beyond man's ways.[24]

---

[24] Isaiah 55:8-9

- You will have clear direction for your life as you keep walking in the light of God. It is God's desire to direct your path and grant you wisdom in knowing His will for your life. The Psalmist speaks of this in Psalm 119:105, 130. *"Your word is a lamp to my feet and a light to my path."* . . . *"The entrance of Your words gives light; It gives understanding to the simple."*

Develop the Bible habit

As you continue reading and studying God's Word, you will find yourself steadily growing in your life as a Christian. The apostle Paul exhorted the church at Colossae to let the word of God be allowed to be a constant part of their life together as followers of Christ. He says to them *"Let the word of Christ dwell in you richly in all wisdom, teaching and admonishing one another in psalms and hymns and spiritual songs, singing with grace in your hearts to the Lord."*

A. Z. Conrad wrote the following prose about the Bible that expresses the confidence of the Christian in the Word of God.

Century follows century – There it stands

Empires rise and fall and are forgotten - There it stands.

Dynasty succeeds dynasty - There it stands.

Kings are crowned and uncrowned - There it stands.

Emperors decree its extermination - There it stands.

Despised and torn to pieces - There it stands.

Storms of hate swirl about it - There it stands.

Atheists rail against it - There it stands.

Agnostics smile cynically - There it stands.

Profane prayerless punsters caricature it - There it stands.

Unbelief abandons it - There it stands.

Higher critics deny its claim to inspiration - There it stands.

Thunderbolts of wrath smite it - There it stands.

An anvil that has broken a million hammers - There it stands.

The flames are kindled about it - There it stands.

The arrows of hate are discharged against it - There it stands.

Radicalism rants and raves about it - There it stands.

Fogs of sophistry conceal it temporarily - There it stands.

The tooth of time gnaws but dents it not - There it stands.

Infidels predict its abandonment - There it stands.

Modernism tries to explain it away - There it stands.

Devotees of folly denounce it - There it stands.

It is God's highway to Paradise.

It is the light on the pathway in the darkest night.

It leads businessmen to integrity and uprightness.

It is the great consoler in bereavement.

It awakens men and women opiated by sin.

It answers every great question of the soul.

It solves every great problem of life.

It is a fortress often attacked but never failing.

Its wisdom is commanding and its logic convincing.

Salvation is its watchword. Eternal life its goal.

It punctures all pretense.

It is forward-looking, outward-looking, and upward-looking.

It out-lives, out-lifts out-loves, out-reaches, out-ranks, out-runs all other books.

Trust it, love it, obey it and Eternal life is yours.[25]

Some study questions for your reflection

1. Why is the Bible different from other books?

2. Why does a Christian need to have a daily time in the Word of God?

3. What are some benefits that accrue to the Christian who disciplines himself to read and study God's Word regularly?

4. What is the difference between the "milk" of the Word of God and the "solid food" of the Word of God?

5. What are some of the practical ways that can help me to read and study God's Word regularly?

6. What can I expect the Word of God to do for me as I spend time in it?

7. Why is it important to read the Bible passage suggested in a devotional guide instead of simply reading the devotional commentary?

---

[25] Gleaned from George Sweeting, Who Said That? (Chicago, IL, Moody Press, 1995) p. 68f.

Chapter 5

Prayer - Developing Intimacy With God!

Prayer is the lifeline of the believer. It is acknowledging God's presence in your life. It is communicating with God while abiding in His grace and love.

Before Adam and Eve sinned by disobeying God's command, they enjoyed an intimate fellowship with God. This relationship is described in Genesis 1 and 2 as God personally walking and talking with them in the garden. God enjoyed fellowship with His creatures until sin disrupted their intimate friendship (Genesis 3:8ff).

Now that you have accepted Christ as your Savior and Lord, your sin has been forgiven and cleansed away. You have been made alive spiritually! This means that your personal relationship with God has been restored. Reading the word of God and praying to God is your means of intimate communication with God, your Heavenly Father, and with Jesus Christ, your Savior and Lord.

God desires your companionship

As His redeemed people, God delights in having us come to Him in prayer. Paul, the apostle, portrays our relationship with God as that of the Heavenly Father with His adopted children. Romans 8:15-17 says

> *For you did not receive the spirit of bondage again to fear, but you received the Spirit of adoption by whom we cry out, 'Abba,[26] Father.' The Spirit Himself bears witness with our spirit that we are children of God, and if children, then heirs - heirs of God and joint heirs with Christ, if indeed we suffer with Him, that we may also be glorified together.*

Now, is that not amazing? The Sovereign God, who created all that exists, could snuff out your life in an instant. Yet this Almighty God wants you to come to Him that you and He might

---

[26] We have already seen in a previous chapter that the word "Abba" is an Aramaic term for father that is better expressed in our English "Papa" or "Daddy."

commune with each other. Isn't it astounding that He cares about every detail of your life and is pleased to be your Friend and your Companion?

God wants you to come with confidence

When we understand that God is awesome in His being, His character and His power, we wonder if we would dare enter into His presence. Whenever the people of Israel saw the glory of God, they were fearful that they would die in His presence. As Moses was receiving the Ten Commandments on Mount Sinai, God's presence was so real that the people feared death because they had seen God. Exodus 20:18-19 says,

> *Now all the people witnessed the thunderings, the lightning flashes, the sound of the trumpet, and the mountain smoking; and when the people saw it, they trembled and stood afar off. Then they said to Moses, "You speak with us, and we will hear; but let not God speak with us, lest we die."*

The writer of Hebrews quells our fear that God is too great to notice us or that God is too busy to be bothered by us. Hebrews 4:14-16 says,

> *Seeing then that we have a great High Priest who has passed through the heavens, Jesus the Son of God, let us hold fast our confession. For we do not have a High Priest who cannot sympathize with our weaknesses, but was in all points tempted as we are, yet without sin. Let us therefore <u>come boldly to the throne of grace</u>, that we may obtain mercy and find grace to help in time of need.*

Christ Jesus, our Savior, has cleared the way for us to come directly into the holy presence of the Almighty God.

To come boldly does not mean to come flippantly or carelessly. We must not treat God casually as "the Man upstairs." The Bible teaches us that we are to "fear" God. In fact, it is the fear of God that is the beginning of real wisdom.[27] To fear the Lord means to come to Him with deep respect and reverence. You are to worship Him and to honor Him with your life. To fear God means to have a healthy inner trembling when you realize that you are privileged to

---

[27] Deuteronomy 10:12; Proverbs 1:7; 3:7; etc.

walk every day in fellowship with Almighty God. To come boldly to God as your Heavenly Father means to come with confidence that you will be received by your Father in heaven who loves you. It means that you can enter into the presence of the Almighty God without fear of being consumed in His presence because Jesus Christ, His Son, has paid the sacrifice for your sin on the cross.

Guards stood outside the office of the king preventing anyone from entering. But a young boy, accompanied by a playmate, passed by the guards and entered the presence of the king. How could he do so? It was because he was the king's son. In a similar way you can now enter the presence of the Holy God because you are now a child of the King, Jesus Christ. You have been purchased by His blood shed on the cross for your sin. Your new relationship with God makes you part of His eternal family.

The pattern of prayer

The disciples asked Jesus to teach them to pray.[28] Matthew gives the more complete account of Jesus teaching His disciples to pray. In Matthew 6:9-13 we find what is commonly referred to as "The Lord's Prayer."

> *In this manner, therefore, pray: Our Father in heaven, Hallowed be Your name. Your kingdom come. Your will be done on earth as it is in heaven. Give us this day our daily bread. And forgive us our debts, as we forgive our debtors. And do not lead us into temptation, But deliver us from the evil one. For Yours is the kingdom and the power and the glory forever. Amen.*

More correctly, this prayer should be called "The Disciples' Prayer." The Lord Jesus could not pray this prayer because, being sinless[29], He could not pray "forgive me my sins." So the Lord Jesus was teaching us how we ought to pray.

While many people recite this prayer word for word, it is really a pattern for prayer. Note the words in verse 9, "*In this manner, therefore, pray.*" You can grow in your prayer intimacy with God as you learn to follow this prayer pattern. It will also help you

---

[28] Luke 11:1-4
[29] Luke's account uses "sins" while Matthew's account uses "debts".

avoid the problem of self-centered praying, bringing only your requests to God. Let's look at the components of this prayer pattern piece by piece.

- **Priority of worship:** Prayer must begin with the worship of God. Worship is our proper response to God's revelation of Himself. We are to recognize the Almighty God as our Father and we are to exalt Him in His glorious Person. *"Our Father in heaven"* addresses God as exalted in heaven while at the same time acknowledging Him as our Father.

"Hallowed be Your name" means that we are to reflect upon Who God is. God's name is to be revered because His name represents all that He is. To "hallow" His name means to "honor as holy" or to "revere as holy." As you hallow His name, reflect on the various attributes of God such as His holiness, His sovereignty, His love, His mercy and grace, His eternal being and His majesty. He is omnipotent (all powerful), omniscient (knows all things from beginning to end), omnipresent (present everywhere). As you grow in your knowledge of God through the Word of God, you will grow in your worship of God.

- **Properly focus your life.** *"Your kingdom come. Your will be done on earth as it is in heaven."* The focus of the life of the Christian should be on doing God's will. The desire of your life ought always to be on God's kingdom. This term *"God's kingdom"* has many aspects of truth for future study. For now, think of God's kingdom as the place where King Jesus rules. Allow Jesus Christ to rule in your life each day. This is the only correct purpose for the believer's life.

Jesus taught us that we are to deny self, take up the cross daily and follow Him.[30] Our focus as Christ's followers is to be upon the day when Christ will return to establish His righteous reign on the earth. This is another aspect of His kingdom or His rule. Until that day, our desire is that His will might be done on this earth in our lives. So begin each day by making certain that your life is focused upon Christ and that you are seeking to walk in fellowship with God. Matthew 6:33 says, *"But seek first the kingdom of God and His righteousness, and all these things shall be added to you."* In Matthew 6:25-32, Jesus speaks about our worrying over the temporal needs of our lives like clothing, food

---

[30] Luke 9:23-26.

and shelter. He assures us that we do not need to worry about these things. Seek the kingdom of God, God's rule in your life, and He will provide for your needs.

- **Personal petitions.** The Lord is concerned about your needs at all times but He wants you to focus upon your needs for today. *"Give us this day our daily bread."* The Lord wants us to be concerned about today, not all the worries of the future. Lehman Strauss says,

"I do at least see here the importance of living one day at a time and trusting God to provide the needs of that one day. By asking for our daily bread, we are simply acknowledging that our times are in God's hands. We do not know what a day will bring forth, but we know the one who does know, and we can go on trusting Him one day at a time."[31]

This is the pattern of prayer and does not restrict us to praying just about food to eat today. I believe the Lord meant that we should be free to come to Him with all of our concerns that are upon our hearts today. It may be concern about our children and their needs, or it may be our concern about a car that is broken down and needs repair. It may be that we are struggling with paying the utility bills or we have health concerns. Whatever our daily needs, we can bring them to the Lord.

- **Request for forgiveness.** *"And forgive us our debts as we forgive our debtors."* Jesus is referring to our debt of sin, as Luke's account makes clear. Luke 11:4 says, *"And forgive us our sins, For we also forgive everyone who is indebted to us."* As a believer, it is very important to keep a clean slate before God. Deal with any sin of which the Holy Spirit convicts you. We need daily forgiveness and cleansing so that we might continue in fellowship with the Father.

By praying this prayer we are reminded of our need to forgive others as they commit sins against us. Christ is teaching us that it is improper to come seeking God to forgive us for our sins if we are not willing to forgive others who have wronged us. The apostle

---

[31] Lehman Strauss, Sense And Nonsense About Prayer (Moody Press, Chicago, 1974) p. 99.

Paul reverses the order as he states that we are to be *"forgiving one another, even as God in Christ forgave you."* [32]

- **Request for victory.** We are not only to seek forgiveness after we have sinned but we are to seek not to fall into new sins. Therefore our Lord instructs us to pray that we might be delivered from temptation and from the snares of the evil one. Does God lead us into temptation? However we interpret this phrase *"lead us not into temptation,"* we know that God never tempts anyone to do evil. James 1:13 says,

> *Let no one say when he is tempted, "I am tempted by God"; for God cannot be tempted by evil, nor does He Himself tempt anyone. But each one is tempted when he is drawn away by his own desires and enticed. Then, when desire has conceived, it gives birth to sin; and sin, when it is full-grown, brings forth death.*

The same word used for "temptation" can refer to God testing us or Satan tempting us. The difference is in the desired result of the testing. God always tests with the intention that we might pass the test and find victory. Satan always tempts with the intent that we might fail, sinning against God. Strauss says "God subjects His children to testing, but Satan seduces them into sin."[33]

- **Recognition of our great God.** Since the translation of the King James Version of the Bible, manuscripts have been discovered that do not include this final sentence, *"For Yours is the kingdom and the power and the glory forever. Amen."* I like this conclusion to the pattern prayer even though the earliest manuscripts may not have included it. The beginning and concluding acknowledgment of God in prayer are like anchoring your prayer time in the very nature and presence of God Himself. In fact, these concluding words remind us of the prayer of David in 1 Chronicles 29:11:

> *Yours, O LORD, is the greatness, The power and the glory, The victory and the majesty; For all that is in heaven and in earth is Yours; Yours is the kingdom, O LORD, And You are exalted as head over all.*

---

[32] Ephesians 4:32
[33] Strauss, Ibid., p. 102

You may tend to be overwhelmed by this pattern of prayer. You may feel that you cannot go through this in detail each time you pray. Don't be concerned about this! Remember that prayer is the experience of acknowledging Christ in your life. Get in the habit of praying about everything. On your way to a special meeting, commit it to the Lord and ask for His wisdom and presence. When you find yourself becoming anxious about some circumstance of life, bring that anxiety to the Lord. You are always in His presence, so you can come to Him always. However, it is a good thing to find some special quiet times, when you can focus on worshiping God. This pattern of prayer will lead you in a meaningful experience of growing in intimacy with God.

Be genuine in prayer

Prayer must always come from the heart. If your heart is right before the Lord, and your life is clean from known sin, the Lord will hear your prayer.

Before He taught them the pattern for prayer, Jesus warned the people against being hypocritical in their religious acts. In Matthew 6:1-4, He warned them about giving their charitable gifts to be seen of men rather than to please God. In verses 5-8, He commanded them not to be like the hypocrites when they pray. He said,

> *And when you pray, you shall not be like the hypocrites. For they love to pray standing in the synagogues and on the corners of the streets, that they may be seen by men. Assuredly, I say to you, they have their reward. But you, when you pray, go into your room, and when you have shut your door, pray to your Father who is in the secret place; and your Father who sees in secret will reward you openly. And when you pray, do not use vain repetitions as the heathen do. For they think that they will be heard for their many words. Therefore do not be like them. For your Father knows the things you have need of before you ask Him.*

Jesus is not saying that we should never pray in public. Public prayer is honoring to the Lord when we are gathered together in a church service to worship the Lord. However, leading in public prayer has its pitfalls for the person praying. One must be in such a relationship with the Lord that he is able to pray genuinely and not for show. He must be consumed with leading the people of God in prayer before the Lord rather than being concerned about how his prayer will sound to the worshipers.

Prayer is never to be a means of showing off our piety or spirituality whether it is public or private prayer. Honesty and humility are the proper attitude for true prayer to Almighty God.

Barriers to effective prayer

The Bible is clear that there are some barriers that prevent God from hearing our prayers. It is useless to pray if God is not listening to us; and if God isn't listening to our prayers, then how can we expect Him to answer our prayers. We need to be certain that all the barriers are cleared away so that God is hearing us.

- **Unconfessed sin.** When God speaks to us about some sin in our lives, we must be willing to deal with that sin. We must forsake it and confess it to the Lord. Then we are assured that the Lord will forgive and cleanse us from our sin.[34]

Psalm 66:18 says, *"If I regard iniquity in my heart, The Lord will not hear."* Therefore it makes no sense to pray when there is unconfessed sin in our hearts. Proverbs 28:13 says, *"He who covers his sins will not prosper, But whoever confesses and forsakes them will have mercy."* When we come to the Lord, we must be sure that we come to Him with clean hands and a pure heart.[35]

- **Selfish motives.** Sometimes we come to the Lord with our requests and God doesn't seem to answer our requests. It may be because we are asking for selfish reasons. The apostle James draws attention to this barrier to effective praying in James 4:2-3: *"Yet you do not have because you do not ask. You ask and do not receive, because you ask amiss, that you may spend it on your pleasures."* There are times when we fail to ask God for what we need. We try to handle it on our own. Other times we do ask but we do not receive an answer because we are self centered in our request. We desire God to answer our request simply to consume it on our selfish pleasures.

---

[34] 1 John 1:9
[35] Psalm 24:3-5

When Jesus prayed in the Garden of Gethsemane, He asked God, the Father, if it were possible to remove the horrible cup of death on the cross from Him. However, after agonizing in prayer, He prayed, *"nevertheless, not as I will, but as You will."* [36] That must be our consuming passion in our lives. "Not my will, LORD, but Your will be done."

- **An unforgiving spirit.** Our relationship with other people must be right or our prayers will be ineffective. Mark 11:25-26 records the words of Jesus on this matter of an unforgiving spirit.

    And whenever you stand praying, if you have anything against anyone, forgive him, that your Father in heaven may also forgive you your trespasses. But if you do not forgive, neither will your Father in heaven forgive your trespasses.

It is impossible to have a right relationship with the Lord if we harbor bitterness, blame or anger toward another person. It is only as we forgive others that the Father will forgive.

- **An improper marriage relationship.** The apostle Peter speaks strongly about the marriage relationship in 1 Peter 3:1-7. He instructs wives about their proper behavior toward husbands who are not yet believers. (Don't keep nagging your husband but live a quiet, peaceable and submissive life that will have great impact upon your unbelieving husband.) In verse 7 husbands are commanded to *"dwell with them according to knowledge, giving honor unto the wife, as unto the weaker vessel, and as being heirs together of the grace of life; that your prayers be not hindered."* Give priority attention to putting into practice biblical truth in your family relationships so your prayers will not be hindered.

- **A wrong mind-set.** It is God's will that each and every believer in Jesus Christ will be dedicated to loving and serving Him and His kingdom's purposes. Matthew 6:33 exhorts us to *"seek first the kingdom of God and His righteousness, and all these things shall be added to you."* We are told by Jesus that we are to pray in His name and whatever we ask in His name, we will

---

[36] Matthew 26:39

receive.[37] So we tack the name of Jesus onto the end of our prayer and then wonder why God doesn't seem to answer our prayer.

What does it mean to pray in Jesus' name? John 15:7-10 explains it further. Jesus said:

> *If you abide in Me, and My words abide in you, you will ask what you desire, and it shall be done for you. By this My Father is glorified, that you bear much fruit; so you will be My disciples. As the Father loved Me, I also have loved you; abide in My love. If you keep My commandments, you will abide in My love, just as I have kept My Father's commandments and abide in His love.*

Praying in the name of Jesus means that we are living in such a close relationship with Him that we want His will more than anything else in our lives. It means that we are abiding in His love and desiring to bear fruit for Him. It means that what He delights in, we also delight in. The Psalmist says in Psalm 37:4, "*Delight yourself also in the LORD, and He shall give you the desires of your heart.*"

Praying according to the will of God

When we pray, we will often feel inadequate in expressing our worship of God. We may be perplexed by certain life situations so that we do not know what is proper to request of God. But we can take heart! God has sent His Holy Spirit into our lives to enable us to pray effectively.

The apostle Paul exhorts us to be "*praying with all prayer and supplication in the Spirit . . .*"[38] The Spirit of God is given to us to enable us to pray effectively. Paul also reminds us of the intercession ministry of the Holy Spirit in Romans 8:26-27:

> *Likewise the Spirit also helps in our weaknesses. For we do not know what we should pray for as we ought, but the Spirit Himself makes intercession for us with groanings which cannot be uttered. Now He who searches the hearts knows what the mind of the Spirit is, because He makes intercession for the saints according to the will of God.*

---

[37] John 14:13-14
[38] Ephesians 6:18

When the Holy Spirit understands our hearts, He takes over for us and intercedes with the Heavenly Father according to the will of God.

We know that God answers our prayers when we are praying according to the will of God. 1 John 5:14-15 is a wonderful promise of God regarding our prayer life. John says:

> *Now this is the confidence that we have in Him, that if we ask anything according to His will, He hears us. And if we know that He hears us, whatever we ask, we know that we have the petitions that we have asked of Him.*

God hears every prayer that is prayed according to the will of God. God answers every prayer that He hears. Therefore, when we pray according to what we know to be the will of God, we know God will answer our prayers. The Word of God will guide us into His truth so that we will be able to measure our prayer requests according to His Word. If we are requesting something that is unmistakably supported by God's Word, then we know we are praying according to God's will.

We need perseverance in developing our prayer life. Satan does his best to keep us from praying or to distract us from our prayer life. We need to set aside special times for prayer when we can be alone with the Lord. It helps us to choose a place where we can speak out loud to God. It helps to keep us from being distracted by other thoughts. Remember what James says in James 5:16: "*. . . The effective, fervent prayer of a righteous man avails much.*"

Some study questions for your reflection

1. In your own words, what would you say prayer is?
2. What gives you the confidence to come into the presence of the Holy God without being rejected or consumed?
3. What does it mean to come boldly to God in prayer?
4. What does it mean to "fear" God? How does this relate to coming boldly to God?
5. In the prayer that Jesus taught His disciples, what are the components of prayer?
6. What are the barriers that get in the way of effective prayer? Are there any of these barriers that you need to deal with right

now in your life?
7. What kinds of prayers will God not hear?
8. What does it mean to pray "in Jesus' name"?
9. How do you know when you are praying according to God's will?

Chapter 6

The Church of Jesus Christ!

When you hear the word "church", how do you react? Depending upon your experiences in local churches, your emotions may be positive or negative.

In the western world, this generation of churches presents a vast array. There are numerous denominations of churches, some of which are faithful to the Bible while others are very liberal in their beliefs. From some pulpits you will hear biblical truth expounded faithfully. From others, you will hear the essentials of the gospel of Jesus Christ rejected, as He is regarded only as a mere man rather than God, the Son. Other churches cannot even be classified as Christian churches because other religions sometimes call their meeting places "churches."

The Lord Jesus Christ said in Matthew 16:18, "*I will build my church . . .*" As you have trusted Jesus Christ as your personal Savior and Lord, you have become a part of His church. This is a great privilege and it also carries responsibility. So let's seek to understand some basic truths about the church of Jesus Christ.

The universal church and local churches

The word "church" comes from the Greek word "ecclesia" which means "the called out ones" or "a called out assembly." This Greek word was used to refer to the people who were called out to vote politically or the people who assembled to conduct the business of their city or town. Jesus used it to refer to His redeemed people who are called out of this world to be His people.

When the Bible speaks of "church," it can refer to either the universal church or the local church. The universal church of Jesus Christ is composed of every truly born again believer on the face of the earth. The universal church also includes all believers who have lived in the past centuries and who have died and gone on to be with the Lord. Some passages in the New Testament that use the word "church" in this way are:

> Matthew 16:18: "*And I also say to you that you are Peter, and on this rock I will build My church, and the gates of Hades shall not prevail against it.*"

> Ephesians 1:22-23: *"And He put all things under His feet, and gave Him to be head over all things to the church, which is His body, the fullness of Him who fills all in all."*
>
> Galatians 1:11: *"For you have heard of my former conduct in Judaism, how I persecuted the church of God beyond measure and tried to destroy it."*

A second use of the word "church" refers to each local body of believers. We often use the word today to refer to the building where people gather to worship God. The New Testament does not emphasize the place but rather the people who, having trusted in Jesus Christ, have been made a part of the body of Jesus Christ on earth. The local church is often referred to as "the church in Jerusalem," "the church in Ephesus" or "the church in Corinth." An example of the local church usage is 1 Corinthians 1:1-3:

> *Paul, called to be an apostle of Jesus Christ through the will of God, and Sosthenes our brother, <u>To the church of God which is at Corinth</u>, to those who are sanctified in Christ Jesus, called to be saints, with all who in every place call on the name of Jesus Christ our Lord, both theirs and ours: Grace to you and peace from God our Father and the Lord Jesus Christ.*

It is essential to distinguish between the universal church and the local churches. The universal church is composed of all truly repentant born-again believers and only they are admitted to the universal church. The local church may be composed of true believers and counterfeit Christians. While every local church ought to insist on having only truly born again believers as members of the church, some churches are very lax on their membership requirements. Even those churches that do insist on this membership standard can sometimes be fooled by a person who professes to have accepted Christ as Savior but who has never truly been born again. So don't be disillusioned when you meet someone in the local church whose lifestyle seems to be totally inconsistent with his profession of faith. He may not be born again or he may be a disobedient believer who needs to get back into fellowship with Christ and His church.

When you accepted Jesus Christ as your Savior and Lord, you were born again by the action of God's Holy Spirit.[39] At the time of your

---

[39] John 3:3-7

salvation you were instated into the universal church of Jesus Christ. This action is described by Paul as the "baptism" of the Holy Spirit. The apostle Paul writes in 1 Corinthians 12:12-13:

> *For as the body is one and has many members, but all the members of that one body, being many, are one body, so also is Christ. For by one Spirit we were all baptized into one body, whether Jews or Greeks, whether slaves or free, and have all been made to drink into one Spirit.*

It is not enough, however, for you to be a member of the universal church of Jesus Christ because the universal church is invisible to a watching world. As a new believer, it is very important for you to seek out a good local church where you can join together with other believers to worship and serve God. Find a church that holds faithfully to the teachings of God's Word, the Bible. Seek out a church where people love Jesus Christ and love each other. If you need help in finding a good biblical local church, write to me [40] and I will seek to give you further guidance.

The beginning of the church

In the Old Testament times, before the coming of Jesus Christ to this earth, the nation of Israel was God's chosen people. Through Abraham and his descendants, God chose to reveal Himself to the world. Jesus, the promised Messiah, came to this world as a Jew, born of the lineage of King David. Jesus was the descendant of Abraham through whom God had promised to bless all nations.[41] The Jews worshiped at the temple in Jerusalem and in local synagogues that were established in most cities and towns wherever a sufficient Jewish population existed.

The church of Jesus Christ was a new entity created by Jesus Christ Himself. The church came into existence through the followers of Jesus Christ and it was established at the time of

---

[40] Write to Dr. Norman P. Anderson, 9619 E. Glencove Circle, Prescott Valley, AZ 86314

[41] Genesis 12:1-3

Pentecost,42 following the death, resurrection and ascension of Jesus Christ. The first local church that was brought into being is in the city of Jerusalem and it was made up of Jewish people who repented and trusted Jesus as their Messiah and Savior. You can read of this event in the second chapter of the book of Acts.

The church at Jerusalem was established in impressive fashion. Through Peter's Spirit-empowered preaching, three thousand Jews repented of their sin and turned in faith to Jesus Christ to be saved. The Holy Spirit was given to them as God's gift (Acts 2:38) and they were added to the disciples of Jesus that day, thus becoming a large local church in the matter of one day. The church in Jerusalem continued to grow rapidly. We read in Acts 2:47 that *"the Lord added to the church daily those who were being saved."*

The functioning of the church

From the beginning of the church in Acts 2, we see the believers functioning as an assembly of people who loved the Lord God and who loved each other. We read about the three thousand new believers in Acts 2:42 – 47:

> *And they continued steadfastly in the apostles' doctrine and fellowship, in the breaking of bread, and in prayers. Then fear came upon every soul, and many wonders and signs were done through the apostles. Now all who believed were together, and had all things in common, and sold their possessions and goods, and divided them among all, as anyone had need. So continuing daily with one accord in the temple, and breaking bread from house to house, they ate their food with gladness and simplicity of heart, praising God and having favor with all the people. And the Lord added to the church daily those who were being saved.*

From this pattern, we discover the essential functions of a local church. If you, as a new believer, devote yourself to these essentials, you will make progress in your Christian life.

---

42 Pentecost was a Jewish festival that dated back to the time of Moses. Pentecost means "fifty days" and it occurred fifty days after Passover. Jesus was crucified on Passover and fifty days later, the Holy Spirit was poured out upon the apostles in a unique fulfillment of the prophecy of Joel. Compare Joel 2:28-32 with Acts 2:17-21.

- **The apostles' doctrine**

The apostles were regularly preaching and teaching the Scriptures to the people. The Scriptures at that time were composed of only the Old Testament books of our Bible. The New Testament was written by the apostles and other first century followers of Christ Jesus. The written Word of God, as we have it in our Bible, did not come merely from human origin but from God Himself. As God moved them along by the Holy Spirit they completed God's written revelation to His people.[43]

You will grow in your knowledge of God and your obedience to God only through systematic and diligent study of the Scriptures. Get in the habit of reading the Bible daily in a systematic way. However, you need also to be taught the word in Bible studies and through the preaching ministry of a dedicated pastor. This is a vital ministry of a faithful local church that is truly serving God.

- **Fellowship**

The word "fellowship" means "sharing." When speaking of Christian fellowship, it signifies much more than simply sharing a meal together or sharing a conversation. It connotes sharing the life of Christ together. It is manifested in sharing the experience of worshiping and serving God together. It means sharing the joys and the sorrows of life together. It refers to being brothers and sisters together in the redeemed family of God. This fellowship involves caring for one another in the love of Christ.

If we are to experience this kind of biblical fellowship, as believers in Christ Jesus, we must commit ourselves to faithful involvement with other Christians. We cannot simply focus upon having others meet our needs; we must seek to be the Lord's instruments to meet the needs of our fellow believers in the local church.

- **The breaking of bread**

The reference to "the breaking of bread" (Acts 2:42) is generally interpreted as a reference to the partaking of the ordinance of the Lord's Supper or communion. The partaking of bread and the cup is based upon Jesus' command to His disciples on the night before His crucifixion when He was betrayed by Judas. At the conclusion

---

[43] 2 Peter 1:19-21; 2 Timothy 3:16-17

of the Passover Supper, Jesus began a new means of remembering Him by commanding his followers to partake regularly of broken bread and a cup of wine.[44] The frequency of partaking of the Lord's Supper varies in local churches. Some churches observe the Lord's Supper every Sunday while others observe it monthly or even less frequently. However often a church observes this important ordinance, it is done in obedience to the command from the Lord to believers to remember Him in His death.

- **Prayers**

Prayer was an integral and important part of the local church. Prayer was like breathing for New Testament believers and it was normal in their corporate gatherings. To pray corporately as well as privately was to confess their total devotion to God and their complete dependence upon God.

In the book of Acts, we find the church often gathered for prayer for some specific needs and in special times of crisis.[45] Learn to pray with and for other believers. Your life will be greatly enriched as you experience answers to your prayers.

- **Mutual care for each other**

The early Christians in the church at Jerusalem were so changed by Jesus Christ that they generously shared what they possessed with other Christians who were in need. Some believe that having all things in common (Acts 2:44) means they sold all their individual possessions and began to live in a commune together. This is not a proper interpretation because verse 46 clearly says that they "broke bread from house to house." They clearly had their own homes but they did sell possessions in order to provide bread (food) for all who were needy. Acts 4:32 comments further in this way: *"Now the multitude of those who believed were of one heart and one soul; neither did anyone say that any of the things he possessed was his own, but they had all things in common."*

---

[44] Further instruction about the Lord's Supper follows in Chapter 8.
[45] A few examples, Acts 1:14 (the church is birthed in prayer); Acts 4:23-31 (the church is empowered and made bold through prayer); Acts 12:5 (prayer for the imprisoned Peter); and Acts 13:1-3 (commissioning missionaries for their work of evangelism); etc.

This view is supported by Dr. John MacArthur's Study Bible. Commenting upon Acts 4:32, MacArthur says:

> "Believers understood that all they had belonged to God, and therefore when a brother or sister had a need those who could meet it were obligated to do so (Cf. James 2:15, 16; 1 John 3:17). The method was to give the money to the apostles who would distribute it (vv. 35, 37)."[46]

The foundation of the church

In Matthew 16:18, Jesus told Peter, "*I also say to you that you are Peter, and on this rock I will build My church, and the gates of Hades shall not prevail against it.*" Who is the rock to whom Jesus is referring?

The Roman Catholic Church teaches that the rock upon which Jesus built His church was Peter and that successive leaders of their denomination are standing in Peter's place as the foundation of the church. But is that what Jesus was saying?

In the Greek language, Peter's name (Petros) meant a small stone but the 'rock' (petra) upon which Jesus would build His church was a huge foundational boulder or rock foundation. In this play on words, Jesus was teaching that the undependable Peter was not a sufficient foundation for His church; rather He Himself would be the only adequate foundation rock upon which His church would stand.

Jesus questioned Peter about his view of Jesus' identity (verses 13-17). Peter answered, "You are the Christ, the Son of the living God." Peter's confession about Christ as the Son of God would be the same testimony given by true believers from then on. Upon such faith in Christ Jesus, Christ's church would be founded.

Peter clearly understood this to be the meaning when he refers to the church in his first letter in 1 Peter 2:4-8.

> *Coming to Him as to a living stone, rejected indeed by men, but chosen by God and precious, you also, as living stones, are being built up a spiritual house, a holy priesthood, to offer up*

---

[46] John MacArthur, The MacArthur Study Bible notes (Word Bibles, Nashville) p. 1641

spiritual sacrifices acceptable to God through Jesus Christ. Therefore it is also contained in the Scripture,

"Behold, I lay in Zion A chief cornerstone, elect, precious, And he who believes on Him will by no means be put to shame." Therefore, to you who believe, He is precious; but to those who are disobedient, "The stone which the builders rejected Has become the chief cornerstone," and "A stone of stumbling And a rock of offense." They stumble, being disobedient to the word, to which they also were appointed.

Like Peter, all believers who confess Jesus Christ to be God, the Son, are built as small living stones into the Lord's church. Jesus Christ, Himself, is the chief cornerstone.

The apostles did have a role in founding the church. They were among the preachers and the missionaries who went everywhere proclaiming the gospel message of Christ crucified and risen again from the dead. They were among the people chosen by God to complete the revelation of God in written Scripture. In this secondary sense, they were the foundation of the church as Paul refers to them in Ephesians 2:20 which says, *". . . having been built upon the foundation of the apostles and prophets, Jesus Christ Himself being the chief cornerstone . . ."*

The expansion of the church

While the church was first founded with Jewish believers in Jerusalem, the church rapidly spread to other communities throughout Palestine. Then it crossed the barriers of prejudice and the gospel was given to the Gentiles. This occurred in fulfillment of Jesus' words in Acts 1:8: *"But you shall receive power when the Holy Spirit has come upon you; and you shall be witnesses to Me in Jerusalem, and in all Judea and Samaria, and to the end of the earth."*

Persecution came upon the Christians in Jerusalem and the Lord used this to spread the gospel to other regions such as Samaria. The powerful witness of believers as they remained faithful to Jesus under their suffering led to the expansion of the church rather than its demise. Acts 8:1-4 speaks of this spreading of the gospel witness of the believers.

> *Now Saul was consenting to his death. At that time a great persecution arose against the church which was at Jerusalem; and they were all scattered throughout the regions of Judea and Samaria, except the apostles. And devout men carried Stephen to his burial, and made great lamentation over him. As for Saul, he made havoc of the church, entering every house, and dragging off men and women, committing them to prison. Therefore those who were scattered went everywhere preaching the word.*

Acts 10 tells the story of Peter going to the house of Cornelius, a Roman military leader. Peter was very prejudiced toward the Gentiles and God had to speak to him emphatically through a vision that came to him three times. God had to convince Peter that it was His sovereign will that the gospel should be preached to the Gentiles as well. When messengers from Cornelius arrived seeking for Peter to come to share God's message with Cornelius, he was ready to go. We read of the results of his preaching to these Gentiles in Acts 10:44-48.

> *While Peter was still speaking these words, the Holy Spirit fell upon all those who heard the word. And those of the circumcision who believed were astonished, as many as came with Peter, because the gift of the Holy Spirit had been poured out on the Gentiles also. For they heard them speak with tongues and magnify God. Then Peter answered, "Can anyone forbid water, that these should not be baptized who have received the Holy Spirit just as we have?" And he commanded them to be baptized in the name of the Lord. Then they asked him to stay a few days.*

The book of Acts is the exciting account of the rapid spread of the gospel throughout the civilized world of that day.

The leadership of the church

The local church cannot function without spiritually minded leaders. From the time of the early church, God's ordained leaders have been pastors or elders. In the places where churches were being established, Paul was concerned that properly qualified elders would be appointed in every local church. In Acts 14:21-23, we find that the apostles appointed qualified leaders in every local church which came into existence through their missionary efforts.

And when they had preached the gospel to that city and made many disciples, they returned to Lystra, Iconium, and Antioch, strengthening the souls of the disciples, exhorting them to continue in the faith, and saying, "We must through many tribulations enter the kingdom of God." So when they had appointed elders in every church, and prayed with fasting, they commended them to the Lord in whom they had believed.

The apostle Paul commands Titus, one of his co-workers to appoint leaders in every local church situation. Titus 1:5 reads, *"For this reason I left you in Crete, that you should set in order the things that are lacking, and appoint elders in every city as I commanded you . . ."*

There are three words used in the New Testament to refer to the same church leaders, "elder," "bishop or overseer" and "pastor or shepherd."[47] "Elder" speaks of the maturity of the men who serve in the vital leadership role of being the pastor of a church. This maturity is not only that which comes from age but also refers to maturity in the person's spiritual life. It is for this reason that a man who served as an elder was not to be a new believer.[48] "Bishop or overseer" refers to the office of the elder that is appointed to provide leadership to the local church. He is to oversee the work of the church. "Shepherd or pastor" refers to the work of taking care of the people of God as a shepherd tends his flock.

The qualifications for bishops (elders, pastors) are given by Paul in 1 Timothy 3:1-7 and Titus 1:5-9. Pastors or elders are to be servant leaders. Jesus taught that anyone who follows Him must seek to be servant of all rather than seeking to be great.[49] The apostle Peter has some forceful words for pastors in 1 Peter 5:1-4:

The elders who are among you I exhort, I who am a fellow elder and a witness of the sufferings of Christ, and also a partaker of the glory that will be revealed: Shepherd the flock of God which is among you, serving as overseers, not by compulsion but willingly, not for dishonest gain but eagerly; nor as being lords over those entrusted to you, but being

---

[47] See Acts 20:17, 28.
[48] 1 Timothy 3:6. (Not a novice or a new convert).
[49] Mark 10:43-45.

examples to the flock; and when the Chief Shepherd appears, you will receive the crown of glory that does not fade away.

A pastor has been given a heavy responsibility to shepherd the flock over which the Lord has made him overseer. He is to do his work conscientiously and he is always to remember that he is a shepherd who serves under the lordship of the Chief Shepherd, Jesus Christ. For this reason, all believers are to obey their leaders. This call to obey the church leaders is not a call to some blind obedience, as if the pastors are infallible human beings; rather it is a call to obey them as those leaders are indeed following Christ Jesus and his clearly revealed word.[50]

Another leader in the church is the deacon which means "servant." In the early days of the church at Jerusalem, a conflict arose over the distribution of food to widows. In Acts 6:3-4, we find the twelve apostles putting the responsibility back upon the congregation to choose out from amongst themselves seven men who were filled with the Holy Spirit and wisdom. These men (deacons) would be in charge of this matter so the apostles could continue to devote themselves to the ministry of the word and to prayer. While Acts 6 does not use the word "deacon," it appears that they were the first appointed deacons in the early church.

Paul also gives qualifications for deacons in I Timothy 3:8-13. These qualifications are similar to those given for bishops or pastors.

The biblical description of the church

There are several metaphors used in Scripture to describe the church of Jesus Christ. Here are five of them.

- **The church as a body**

The apostle Paul describes the church as a body of believers. In 1 Corinthians 12 Paul teaches that the Holy Spirit gives different gifts, abilities and functions to the individual believers who make up the church. In verses 12-31 of this chapter, he uses the human body to illustrate how the body of Christ must function. As the human body is made up of many different members with different functions, so the body of Christ, the church, is composed

---

[50] Hebrews 13:7, 17

of many different members who are gifted as the Holy Spirit wills. As the members of the body must not seek prominence or seek to operate independently of each other, so it is in the church, the body of Christ. As each member of the church body serves his or her purpose and as each member works cooperatively for the good of the body, unity in the body is achieved.

- **The church as a flock of sheep**

In John 10, Jesus begins this metaphor by calling Himself the Good Shepherd. He says in John 10:11, 14:

> *"I am the good shepherd. The good shepherd gives His life for the sheep. . . I am the good shepherd; and I know My sheep, and am known by My own."* Again in verse 27, Jesus says, *"My sheep hear My voice, and I know them, and they follow Me. . ."*

In 1 Peter 5:2, he exhorts the elders or pastors to *"Shepherd the flock of God which is among you, serving as overseers . . ."*

This imagery of the flock and the Shepherd reminds us of Psalm 23, one of the most loved Psalms, where David begins his Psalm with *"The Lord is my Shepherd, I shall not want."*

- **The church as a family**

In Ephesians 2:19, the apostle Paul refers to the family of believers as *"members of the household of God."* Galatians 6:10 says *"Therefore, as we have opportunity, let us do good to all, especially to those who are of the household of faith."*

The concept of being part of the family of God is found throughout the New Testament. All believers in Jesus Christ, male and female, are included in the term "sons of God" as we have been adopted into God's redeemed family. Romans 8:14-17 is a thrilling passage of Scripture that informs us of this loving family relationship we have in Christ Jesus.

> *For as many as are led by the Spirit of God, these are sons of God. For you did not receive the spirit of bondage again to fear, but you received the Spirit of adoption by whom we cry out, "Abba, Father." The Spirit Himself bears witness with our spirit that we are children of God, and if children, then*

heirs - heirs of God and joint heirs with Christ, if indeed we suffer with Him, that we may also be glorified together.

We are privileged to call Almighty God *"Father."* When we have accepted the salvation provided through Jesus Christ, our Savior and Lord, we are included in this personal relationship with God as our Heavenly Father.

We also have a personal relationship with all other believers. Throughout the New Testament, other believers are referred to as brothers. As children in God's family, we are to practice love for one another as brothers and sisters in Christ Jesus. 1 John 3:10-11 speaks strongly to us of this matter.

In this the children of God and the children of the devil are manifest: Whoever does not practice righteousness is not of God, nor is he who does not love his brother. For this is the message that you heard from the beginning, that we should love one another . . .

The apostle Peter also instructs us in 1 Peter 3:8-9:

Finally, all of you be of one mind, having compassion for one another; love as brothers, be tenderhearted, be courteous; not returning evil for evil or reviling for reviling, but on the contrary blessing, knowing that you were called to this, that you may inherit a blessing.

- **The church as a building or temple**

A common way of looking at the church building is to see it as God's house, a place where God dwells. God is present in the church building, or anywhere else, whenever two or three are gathered in His name.[51] God's dwelling place is in His redeemed people. Ephesians 2:19-22 says:

Now, therefore, you are no longer strangers and foreigners, but fellow citizens with the saints and members of the household of God, having been built on the foundation of the apostles and prophets, Jesus Christ Himself being the chief cornerstone, in whom the whole building, being fitted together, grows into a holy temple in the Lord, in whom you

---

[51] Matthew 18:20

also are being built together for a dwelling place of God in the Spirit.

Each individual believer is a temple of the Holy Spirit.[52] In 1 Corinthians 3:16-17, the apostle Paul also speaks of the corporate church made up of all true believers as the temple of God, the dwelling place of God by His Spirit.

> *Do you not know that you are the temple of God and that the Spirit of God dwells in you? If anyone defiles the temple of God, God will destroy him. For the temple of God is holy, which temple you are."*[53]

- **The church as the bride of Christ**

The Old Testament prophets spoke frequently about the relationship of God and His chosen people, Israel, as like that of the bridegroom and the bride. God delighted in His people and desired that they might be a pure bride and wife to Him. In Isaiah 62:5, we read, *"And as the bridegroom rejoices over the bride, so shall your God rejoice over you."*[54]

In the New Testament, the church of Jesus Christ is seen as the bride being prepared for her Bridegroom, Jesus Christ. In Ephesians 5:22-33, the apostle Paul teaches about the proper relationship of husband and wife in marriage. He compares the pure relationship between husband and wife as the relationship between Christ and His church. In verse thirty, he reminds us that we are all members of His body. In verse 31, he says *"This is a great mystery, but I speak concerning Christ and the church."*

Jesus shares a parable of ten virgins who are waiting for the bridegroom to come as a picture of His people waiting for His return at the end of the age.[55] This is taken from the wedding practices of the Jews in Jesus' time. The bride was engaged to be married to the bridegroom in an arranged marriage. The bridegroom was diligently preparing the place where he and his

---

[52] 1 Corinthians 6:19-20 speaks of the body of each believer as the temple of God's Holy Spirit, purchased at great cost by the blood of Jesus Christ.
[53] The pronoun "you" is plural in these verses, meaning the corporate body of believers, the church.
[54] See also Isaiah 61:10
[55] Matthew 25:1-13

bride would live. He would not come to marry his bride until his home was prepared. The bride did not know exactly when that day would be, however, she, and her friends, were waiting in anticipation and in readiness for that day. Then the bridegroom would come, the wedding would be celebrated, and the bridegroom would take his bride to his home. Matthew 25:13 gives us the primary message of the parable. *"Watch therefore, for you know neither the day nor the hour in which the Son of Man is coming."*

In a similar manner, Jesus is preparing a place for His bride, the church. Someday He will return to take His bride to himself in heaven, in that New Jerusalem, where He and His bride, the church will be together forever and forever. We, as His redeemed people, the church, are to keep ourselves pure and ready for His call to us to come to His marriage supper. You may take your Bible and read many other references to Christ as the Bridegroom and His bride the church in the book of Revelation.[56]

As a part of His bride, the church, we are to keep ourselves pure ourselves in an ungodly world until the Bridegroom comes to call us home to be with Him forever.

The mission of the church

The Lord Jesus commissioned His disciples before He returned to heaven. Acts 1:8 reads *"But you shall receive power when the Holy Spirit has come upon you; and you shall be witnesses to Me in Jerusalem, and in all Judea and Samaria, and to the end of the earth."* The commission is for all believers, all who follow Jesus. If others are going to know the good news that Jesus Christ will give them eternal life through faith alone in Him alone, it is imperative that we faithfully share the message with them. Matthew 28:18-20 gives us "The Great Commission."

> *And Jesus came and spoke to them, saying, "All authority has been given to Me in heaven and on earth. Go therefore and make disciples of all the nations, baptizing them in the name of the Father and of the Son and of the Holy Spirit, teaching them to observe all things that I have commanded*

---

[56] Revelation 19:6-9; 21:2-3; 21:9-10

> *you; and lo, I am with you always, even to the end of the age."*

If you were passing by a house and noticed that it was on fire, would you not go to the door and seek to arouse those who may be sleeping there? Would you not do your best to make them aware of the danger, urging them with passion to get out of the burning building? When the souls of people are in danger of spending eternity in hell with no hope of ever escaping, will you not warn them? When these same people can be offered immediate forgiveness of sin and the gift of eternal life in heaven, do you not want to be involved in giving them that "good news"?

Ask the pastor of the church you have chosen to attend if the church trains their people in evangelism. Get involved in learning how to share the gospel effectively.

The unity of the church

It is the Lord's will that His church be in harmony and unity. Unity does not mean uniformity. It is healthy to have different viewpoints on many things. However, it is paramount to be unified on the essentials of the faith. Unity also requires that we have tolerance for the views of others on the non-essentials.

Jesus talked much about the need for His followers to love one another. In fact, our effectiveness in our mission is dependent upon our love for one another. In John 13:34-35, Jesus plainly tell us:

> *"A new commandment I give to you, that you love one another; as I have loved you, that you also love one another. By this all will know that you are My disciples, if you have love for one another."*

In Ephesians 4:1-6, the apostle Paul exhorts the church at Ephesus:

> *I, therefore, the prisoner of the Lord, beseech you to walk worthy of the calling with which you were called, with all lowliness and gentleness, with longsuffering, bearing with one another in love, endeavoring to keep the unity of the Spirit in the bond of peace. There is one body and one*

> *Spirit, just as you were called in one hope of your calling; one Lord, one faith, one baptism; one God and Father of all, who is above all, and through all, and in you all.*

Note the list of essential beliefs upon which we must agree. To depart from what the Bible teaches in these essentials is to fracture the church through false doctrines. However, unity means that we are peacemakers and we do not insist on making non-essential issues "bones of contention." We seek to keep the unity of the Spirit in the church.

Your involvement in a church

When you trusted Christ Jesus as your Savior and were granted eternal life by God, you entered a personal relationship with Jesus Christ. You also entered into the corporate family of God and became a part of God's new community of redeemed people. Therefore it is important for you to seek out a local church body where you can commit yourself to worship and serve God along with other believers who are seeking to obey Jesus Christ.

The writer of Hebrews gives us a strong exhortation to consistent involvement in the local church body so that we might be growing responsible followers of Jesus Christ. In Hebrews 10:23-25, we read:

> *Let us hold fast the confession of our hope without wavering, for He who promised is faithful. And let us consider one another in order to stir up love and good works, not forsaking the assembling of ourselves together, as is the manner of some, but exhorting one another, and so much the more as you see the Day approaching.*

No local church is perfect since imperfect members like you and I make up the church. However, we are in the process of being perfected in Christ Jesus. Someday we will be like Him for we will see Him as He is.[57] Until Christ Jesus, our Perfect Savior and Lord, calls us home, we must commit ourselves to being faithful members of a local church that is preaching and teaching the word of God. As Charles Colson says:

---

[57] 1 John 3:2

"... following the pattern made normative in the Book of Acts, each believer is to make his or her confession, be baptized, and become part of a local congregation with all of the accountability that implies. So membership in a church particular is no more optional than membership in the church universal."[58]

Some study questions for your reflection

1. According to Scripture, what is the universal church of Jesus Christ?
2. When and how did you become a member of the universal church of Jesus Christ?
3. When did Jesus establish His church? Where do we read of this event in the Bible?
4. What is the difference between a local church and the universal church?
5. Who is the foundation of the universal church?
6. What are the biblical functions of a local church that ought to be primary in the local church's ministry to believers?
7. What responsibility does each church have toward those who are not yet believers? In other words, what should the mission of each local church be?
8. Who are the biblically defined leaders of a local church? What is the responsibility of each member toward these leaders?
9. If a church leader is violating the standards of Scripture in his life style, do you have a responsibility to follow and obey these leaders? Why or why not?
10. How should I choose a good biblical local church in which to become involved?
11. Of the various metaphors that the Bible uses to describe the church, which is most meaningful to you? Why?

---

[58] Charles Colson, The Body (Word Publishing, Dallas. London. Vancouver. Melbourne, 1992) p. 70

Chapter Seven

Understanding Baptism - Your Public Proclamation of Faith!

You'll find in your Christian life that baptism is one of the most controversial subjects you will encounter. This wide range of views causes confusion to reign in the minds of many. Therefore it is important to go directly to the New Testament Scriptures to seek to understand what the Bible teaches. God's revealed teaching is of primary importance and takes precedence over church traditions.

As a new believer in Jesus Christ, you may have some church background or you may come from a totally un-churched background. If you have been raised in a church that has taught some other view than what you see in this chapter, you may struggle with accepting what the Bible clearly teaches. I understand the struggle. Adopting the biblical teachings about baptism may require changing some of your childhood teaching. Then you'll wonder about disowning your heritage and your family ties. Study the Scriptures for yourself and pray that the Holy Spirit will teach you God's truth as found in the Bible.

What does baptism accomplish?

In New Testament times, when the church was in its very early stages of development, baptism occurred almost immediately after a person's new birth experience. When a person professed his faith in Christ's death and resurrection as his means of salvation, he soon followed that profession with his baptism in water as a public proclamation of his faith.

Baptism does not save us from our sin. Baptism is a public testimony of your trust in Christ's death, burial and resurrection as the means of salvation. If one has not been born again by faith in Jesus Christ, then baptism has no meaning whatsoever. Dr. Millard Erickson says:

> "The act of baptism conveys no direct spiritual benefit or blessing. In particular, we are not regenerated through baptism, for baptism presupposes faith and the salvation to which faith leads. It is, then a testimony that one has already been regenerated. If there is a spiritual benefit, it is

the fact that baptism brings us into membership or participation in the local church."[59]

However, some churches teach that baptism is the means of saving a person from his sin. Others believe that it is a sign of God's covenant, that it is a parallel to circumcision under the Old Covenant.[60] As such, they see infant baptism as valid because circumcision was performed on Jewish male children at eight days of age.

As a result of these teachings, many people have a false assurance of being on their way to heaven because they have been baptized either as an infant or an adult. While a casual reading of some passages may seem to teach that salvation comes through baptism, a thorough study of these passages will show that a person is saved by faith alone in Jesus Christ alone. It is the blood of Jesus Christ that cleanses from all sin, not baptism. In Hebrews 9:22, the writer of Hebrews clearly states "... *without the shedding of blood there is no remission."* Scripture makes it clear that salvation comes only through faith in Jesus Christ and His death on the cross in our behalf. It is the blood of Jesus that cleanses from all sin. 1 Peter 1:17-19 says:

> *"And if you call on the Father, who without partiality judges according to each one's work, conduct yourselves throughout the time of your stay here in fear; knowing that you were not redeemed with corruptible things, like silver or gold, from your aimless conduct received by tradition from your fathers, but with the precious blood of Christ, as of a lamb without blemish and without spot."*

I have been to many funerals in some of these churches that teach salvation comes from baptism. The pastor or priest will emphatically declare that the person is in heaven because he or she was baptized. How sad, to give such assurance to the family, when the Scriptures offer no such assurance. Many people who accept such a belief system show no evidence of a spiritual rebirth. They are like the Pharisees and Sadducees of Jesus day who

---

[59] Millard J. Erickson, Christian Theology, Vol. 3 (Baker Book House, Grand Rapids, Michigan, 1985) p 1096
[60] For further study of these views, see Millard J. Erickson, IBID, pp 1089-1105

believed they were right with God because of the rituals they observed.

One passage of Scripture that does seem to teach that baptism saves us is found in 1 Peter 3:18-22. However, the question is: From what does baptism save us? Does it save us from sin and give us eternal life? Or is Peter speaking about something else?

> *For Christ also suffered once for sins, the just for the unjust, that He might bring us to God, being put to death in the flesh but made alive by the Spirit, by whom also He went and preached to the spirits in prison, who formerly were disobedient, when once the Divine longsuffering waited in the days of Noah, while the ark was being prepared, in which a few, that is, eight souls, were saved through water. There is also an antitype* (means 'symbol') *which now saves us, baptism (not the removal of the filth of the flesh, but the answer of a good conscience toward God), through the resurrection of Jesus Christ, who has gone into heaven and is at the right hand of God, angels and authorities and powers having been made subject to Him.*

In verse 21, Peter tells us that baptism is *"the answer of a good conscience toward God, through the resurrection of Jesus Christ . . ."* Moffatt has translated it, *"a prayer to God for a clear conscience. . ."* Thus, baptism saves us from an evil conscience because baptism is a prayer to God for a clear conscience upon the basis of faith in Christ's death and resurrection and because of obedience to the commandment of our Lord. The believer, in his baptism, is saying in essence to God: "Father, I have placed my faith and trust in Jesus Christ, your Son. I am depending only upon His death and burial and resurrection as the means of my salvation. I have done all that you require of me. Now I ask for a clear conscience before You."

Baptism is an initiatory rite to the local church and it is to be obediently entered only after one has been born again through repentance and faith in our Lord Jesus Christ.

The command to be baptized

Jesus Christ did not baptize anyone Himself but He did command that all who claim to be His disciples should be baptized. We find this command stated in the Great Commission in Matthew 28:18-20.

> *And Jesus came and spoke to them, saying, "All authority has been given to Me in heaven and on earth. Go therefore and make disciples of all the nations, baptizing them in the name of the Father and of the Son and of the Holy Spirit, teaching them to observe all things that I have commanded you; and lo, I am with you always, even to the end of the age.*

This passage of Scripture requires some study. The main verb is not clear in the English translation; however, in the original Greek, it is clear. The main verb is "make disciples." All the rest of the verb forms in this command are participles that relate to the main verb. The command from Jesus is that we are to be about the work of making disciples or followers of Jesus. Then we are to baptize and teach them, that is, those who have become His followers.

It is plain to see that salvation does not come from being baptized but from becoming His disciples (followers). We become disciples by repenting from our sin and trusting what Christ has done for us through His death on the cross and His resurrection from the dead.

When you repent and put your faith in Jesus Christ, you become a follower (disciple) of Jesus Christ. Baptism is a primary step of obedience to Christ after you have trusted Christ as your Savior. Are you willing to obey Christ's command by being baptized? This is God's intended way for you to make a public proclamation of your faith in Christ Jesus.

In the New Testament church, baptism was so widely accepted as the normal first step of obedience for new believers that Peter commanded the new believers in Cornelius's household to be baptized (Acts 10:48). Peter did not leave baptism as an option for Cornelius and his believing friends.

The mode and meaning of baptism

Some people find it unimportant to discuss the mode of baptism because, in their opinion, it matters little whether the baptism water is administered by sprinkling, pouring or immersion. But, again, we must turn to the Scriptures. Romans 6:3-6 teaches that baptism is the means of declaring one's identity with the death, burial and resurrection of Jesus Christ. The immersion mode of baptism best expresses this meaning.

> *Or do you not know that as many of us as were baptized into Christ Jesus were baptized into His death? Therefore we were buried with Him through baptism into death, that just as Christ was raised from the dead by the glory of the Father, even so we also should walk in newness of life. For if we have been united together in the likeness of His death, certainly we also shall be in the likeness of His resurrection, knowing this, that our old man was crucified with Him, that the body of sin might be done away with, that we should no longer be slaves of sin.*

Baptism by immersion is a striking object lesson of Christ's death, burial and resurrection as our only means of salvation. When you are lowered beneath the water, this act expresses death and burial, signifying that you have, by faith, accepted the death of Christ as your own. When you are raised from the water, this act expresses resurrection to your new life in Christ. You are expressing, by your baptism, your faith in the resurrection of Jesus Christ as your only means of eternal life. Because Christ Jesus lives, you also live.

Our English word "baptize" is a transliteration, rather than a translation of the Greek word "baptizo." This means that translators have simply coined a new English word that sounds like the Greek word. Any Greek to English lexicon (dictionary) shows clearly that the basic translation of "baptize" is "to dip, to immerse, to submerge, to overwhelm."[61] Translators and Bible publishers continue to use "baptize" instead of "immerse" in order to avoid controversy and to make their translations of the Bible acceptable to all churches.

As John, the Baptist, was baptizing people, it is clear that it was by immersion. In Matthew 3:6 we find that many people were being "baptized" (immersed) by him in the Jordan, confessing their sins. When Jesus was baptized by John, we read that Jesus "came up immediately from (out of) the water . . ." Most Bible

---

[61] For example, check out Thayer's Greek-English Lexicon of the New Testament (Zondervan Publishing House, Grand Rapids, Michigan) p. 94.

scholars agree that the New Testament teaches baptism by immersion and that the modes of sprinkling and pouring were adopted at a later time in church history.

Who should be baptized?

Scripture plainly shows that only those who have repented from their sin and have placed their faith in Jesus Christ as Savior and Lord are to be baptized. Those who have become followers of Jesus Christ are to be baptized. We have already seen this from the Great Commission in Matthew 28:18-20. In Acts 2:41, we find it was *"those who gladly received his word were baptized . . ."* In the book of Acts we have examples of believers being immersed in water as a public proclamation of their faith in Jesus Christ. Read passages like Acts 8:26-40; 9:1-19; 10:44-48; 16:13-15 and 16:16-34. For someone to be baptized without first of all repenting and trusting Christ Jesus as Savior is meaningless.

The Bible teaches believer's baptism. This does not necessarily mean adult baptism. Children and youth are subjects for baptism providing they meet the conditions for baptism. Can they give evidence of a changed life that has been brought about by true repentance and genuine faith in Jesus Christ as Lord and Savior? Dr. Millard J. Erickson says: "Scripture makes it clear that personal, conscious faith in Christ is prerequisite to baptism."[62]

Many churches practice the baptism of infants, some churches by sprinkling or pouring, other churches by immersion. Infant baptism is not taught in the Bible. Infant baptism arises out of the mistaken belief that baptism washes away a person's sins and grants them eternal life. Some seek to argue that household baptisms in the book of Acts, such as the Philippian jailor in Acts 16:16-34, must have included infants. However, careful study of the passage shows that he and his household were baptized (verse 33) but also he and his entire household believed in God (verse 34).

As a pastor of forty years, it has been my practice to baptize believing children who have reached the age of twelve years. I have resisted the pressure of parents to baptize their younger

---

[62] Millard J. Erickson, IBID, p. 1097

children. I fear that some pastors who profess to hold to believers' baptism border upon infant baptism or at least toddler baptism by baptizing very young children. When children as young as three or four years are baptized, it seems questionable that one so young finds baptism a significant expression of repentance and faith. Such a baptism is more likely motivated by the pressure of a parent or a pastor.

What biblical basis is there for insisting that children be at least twelve years of age to qualify for baptism? I admit there is no definitive statement in Scripture on this matter. However, I believe that we must consider the historical context of baptism in the New Testament. The early church was formed out of the Jewish heritage. Our Jewish friends regard their children as having accepted adult responsibility when they enter their teen years. Jesus' parents brought Him to the temple at the age of twelve to celebrate Passover (Luke 2:41-52). Given this Jewish heritage, I question that the leaders of the early church baptized anyone under the age of twelve.

The baptism of John, the Baptist

John, the Baptist, was the forerunner of Christ, the Messiah, and as such, sought to prepare the way of the Messiah so that He would be accepted and received by the people. In Matthew 3:1-10, we have a clear account of John's ministry. In verses 2 and 3, we see that his message was a message of repentance so that the people might *"prepare the way of the LORD. . ."* In Acts 19:4-5, the apostle Paul, referred to John's baptism as *"the baptism of repentance"* and he contrasts it with being *baptized in the name of the Lord Jesus."*

The word "repent" means "to change one's mind." A change of mind regarding the Messiah, on the part of the Jews, involved a change of action. To indicate one's willingness to turn from self-centered sinful living and to receive the promised Messiah upon His arrival, John required that one submit to immersion in water. The Jamieson, Fausett and Brown Bible Commentary gives the following explanation of repentance.

> "Though the word strictly denotes a change of mind, it has respect here, and wherever it is used in connection with salvation, primarily to that sense of sin which leads a sinner

to flee from wrath to come, to look for relief only from above, and eagerly to fall in with the provided remedy."[63]

John, the Baptist, clearly was agitated by some of the Pharisees and the Sadducees who were coming for baptism but were not displaying sincere repentance (Matthew 3:7-9). Baptism as a rite without repentance has no validity. Baptism has never been a sacrament, dispensing the grace and forgiveness of God through the act itself.

The requirement of Jewish people to be immersed in water was a new thing for the Jews. Jamieson, Fausset and Brown say:

> "The baptism itself startled, and was intended to startle them. They were familiar enough with the baptism of proselytes from heathenism; but this baptism of Jews themselves was quite new and strange to them."

The baptism by John had a common significance with Christian baptism in that both speak of death and resurrection. John's baptism was prophetic, looking forward to the death and resurrection of the Messiah, an idea which to the Jewish mind was unacceptable. Note Peter's response in Matthew 16:21-23 when Jesus attempted to teach them of His impending suffering and death.

> *From that time Jesus began to show to His disciples that He must go to Jerusalem, and suffer many things from the elders and chief priests and scribes, and be killed, and be raised the third day. Then Peter took Him aside and began to rebuke Him, saying, "Far be it from You, Lord; this shall not happen to You!" But He turned and said to Peter, "Get behind Me, Satan! You are an offense to Me, for you are not mindful of the things of God, but the things of men.*

While John's baptism looked forward to Christ's death and resurrection, believer's baptism looks back upon the historical death and resurrection of Christ.

The baptism of Jesus

---

[63] Jamieson, Faucet and Brown, (Three volume set; Bible Commentary) Vol. 3, p. 10

The baptism of Jesus by John, the Baptist, is very often treated casually as if it had very little significance. When you read Matthew 3:11-17, you must conclude that Jesus regarded His baptism of great importance.

> *Then Jesus came from Galilee to John at the Jordan to be baptized by him. And John tried to prevent Him, saying, "I need to be baptized by You, and are You coming to me?" But Jesus answered and said to him, "Permit it to be so now, for thus it is fitting for us to fulfill all righteousness." Then he allowed Him.*
>
> *When He had been baptized, Jesus came up immediately from the water; and behold, the heavens were opened to Him, and He saw the Spirit of God descending like a dove and alighting upon Him. And suddenly a voice came from heaven, saying, "This is My beloved Son, in whom I am well pleased."*

In verse 15 Jesus states that, in some way, all righteousness was being fulfilled through His baptism by John. The question of importance is "what did Jesus mean by that statement?"

We may partially find our answer in analyzing the events that corresponded to the baptism of Jesus. It was His baptism that launched the three years of His public ministry. The baptism of Jesus was also the means of unmistakably identifying the Messiah to John. In John 1:29-34, we read:

> *The next day John saw Jesus coming toward him, and said, "Behold! The Lamb of God who takes away the sin of the world! This is He of whom I said, 'After me comes a Man who is preferred before me, for He was before me.' I did not know Him; but that He should be revealed to Israel, therefore I came baptizing with water." And John bore witness, saying, "I saw the Spirit descending from heaven like a dove, and He remained upon Him. I did not know Him, but He who sent me to baptize with water said to me, 'Upon whom you see the Spirit descending, and remaining on Him, this is He who baptizes with the Holy Spirit.' And I have seen and testified that this is the Son of God."*

John proclaimed that the coming Messiah would baptize with the Holy Spirit and with fire (Matthew 3:11-12). Jesus could produce the new birth through the Holy Spirit (John 3:5). Through the spiritual new birth, inward cleansing and purity becomes a reality. It was following John's baptism of Jesus and his witnessing of the accompanying signs (John 1:33) that John announced to his disciples, *"Behold the Lamb of God, who takes away the sin of the world" (John 1:29).*

The baptism of Jesus was not merely to identify with sinful men, although He did that at Calvary when He was made sin for us (2 Corinthians 5:21). Nor was He simply setting an example for all who would believe in Him. The baptism of Jesus was a public pronouncement that He was the promised Messiah and that He was fulfilling His Messianic mission assigned to Him by the Heavenly Father. The descent of the Holy Spirit in the form of a dove and the voice of the Father from heaven supported this claim. George Beasley- Murray says:

> "The baptism of Jesus takes on a fuller significance from this viewpoint. Far from being a simple acceptance of the death sentence it indicates the initiation of the divine intervention, the downfall of the powers of darkness, the dawn of the new creation, the promise of life from the dead! And this, indeed, is the spirit in which Jesus departed the Jordan." [64]

A brief interpretation of church history

As you have studied through the Scriptures to see what they teach about baptism, you may be asking, "When this is so clear in Scripture, what happened to lead to all the present day confusion?" A very brief interpretation of church history may be helpful.

The first movement away from immersion as the mode of baptism seems to have come with the introduction of "clinic baptism" by pouring in the case of one who is ill and unable to be immersed. Pouring was allowed in "THE DIDACHE" (didache means 'teachings') an early church document dated 130 - 160 A.D.

---

[64] George Beasley-Murray, Baptism In the New Testament (Macmillan & Co. Ltd., London, England, 1962) p. 61.

The major step away from the truth of New Testament teaching was the intrusion of the doctrine of "baptismal regeneration". The teaching that baptism was the means of receiving God's grace and forgiveness appeared by 150-200 A.D. and grew in magnitude rather rapidly. Cyprian, bishop of Carthage, 249-258 A.D., formalized the baptism of new-born infants, claiming that their baptism removed original sin from them. Pope Gregory I, 604 A.D., was the first to draw up a liturgy for the baptism of infants. Sprinkling as a mode of baptism was not introduced until the thirteenth century and was formalized by the Council of Ravenna in 1311 A.D.

The Anabaptists arose in the sixteenth century as a group of reformers who were considered fanatics, schismatics, and a menace by both the Roman Catholics and the Lutherans. They were called "Anabaptist" as an epithet because of their "re-baptizing" of believers. They became true believers through reading the Scriptures for themselves and they rejected their infant baptism as being unscriptural. The Anabaptists are the forerunners of the Mennonites and the Baptists. For an interesting survey of this part of history, you may read chapters two and three of 'A History of the Baptists' by Robert G. Torbet.[65]

If you have recently trusted Christ Jesus as your Savior or you have been a believer for a long time, but have never followed obediently in the waters of baptism, then I encourage you to take this step now. Contact your pastor and arrange to be immersed in water, in obedience to the command of Jesus Christ, your Savior.

Some study questions for your reflection

1. Did you have any church background as a child? What were you taught that baptism meant?
2. According to Scripture, what does baptism mean? In what ways does baptism speak of your identification with Jesus Christ?

---

[65] Robert G. Torbet, A History of the Baptists, Judson Press, Chicago, 1950)

3. What is the English meaning of the Greek word 'baptizo' or the English word 'baptize'?
4. According to Scripture, who qualifies to be baptized?
5. What was the significance of the baptism administered by John, the Baptist?
6. Why was Jesus baptized?
7. How did John, the Baptist, know that Jesus was the promised Messiah and Savior of the world?
8. Should young children, who have trusted Christ as Savior, be baptized? What do you think of the historical context argument for baptizing children only as they reach the age of twelve?
9. Have you been baptized yet as a believer? If not, are you willing to take this step of obedience to Jesus Christ?

Chapter Eight

The Lord's Supper: Remembering Our Lord!

Jesus commanded Christians to practice two symbolic ceremonies. We studied the first one, baptism, in chapter seven. The second one is known as the Lord's Supper. Through baptism the new believer announces his faith in Christ publicly and is initiated into the local church. It is observed only once. The Lord's Supper is a repeated ordinance that every believer is commanded to observe as a means of remembering the death of Jesus on the cross. While baptism symbolizes the beginning of the Christian life, the Lord's Supper symbolizes the continuance of the Christian life.

Some churches call baptism and the Lord's Supper sacraments, because they believe that they convey God's grace to man. But we do not receive eternal life and forgiveness of our sin from God either by means of water baptism or the Lord's Supper. The New Testament declares that we are saved by faith alone in Christ alone. We are saved by trusting Jesus Christ as Savior and Lord and by trusting His death on the cross and His resurrection from the dead as our means of being declared right in God's sight (Ephesians 2:8,9).

Some other terms for the Lord's Supper

Many churches will refer to the Lord's Supper as communion. The apostle Paul refers to the Lord's Supper as "communion" in 1 Corinthians 10:16-17.

> *The cup of blessing which we bless, is it not the communion of the blood of Christ? The bread which we break, is it not the communion of the body of Christ? For we, though many, are one bread and one body; for we all partake of that one bread.*

The Lord's Supper speaks of the vertical relationship that is established through Jesus Christ between the newly born-again believer and God, the Father. We are brought into a personal relationship with God through what Jesus Christ did for us on the cross. He bore our sins and paid the penalty for our sin completely. Because His shed blood is the atoning blood for our sins, we are declared to be in a right relationship with God through faith. The Bible refers to this as being justified before God by the blood of Christ Jesus.[66]

The Lord's Supper also speaks of another dimension of communion. We who are trusting Christ as Savior have communion horizontally with our brothers and sisters in the family of God. The Holy Spirit dwells in every true believer, giving us a special communion with other true believers.

Some churches refer to the Lord's Supper as the Eucharist. Eucharist comes from a Greek word meaning "thanksgiving." The Lord's Supper is a time of giving thanks to Jesus Christ for dying for our sins, for bearing our guilt for us on the cross.

The Passover and the Lord's Supper

As Jews, Jesus and His disciples faithfully celebrated the Passover. The Passover is a time of remembrance for all Jewish people of faith. It was a feast of the Jews that was observed once a year to remind them of God's miraculous deliverance from slavery in Egypt. Moses was God's instrument to lead the people out of Egypt. On the final night in Egypt, God broke Pharaoh's resistance by sending the death angel to strike dead the firstborn son of every household in Egypt. The Jews were commanded to kill an unblemished lamb and apply the blood of the lamb to the doorframes of their homes. As the death angel saw the applied blood, he would pass over that home and the first born son was saved.[67] What a picture this is of Jesus Christ, the Lamb of God who spares us from God's judgment when His shed blood is applied to our hearts by faith.

On the last Passover night before His death on the cross, Jesus directed His disciples to make preparations so they could observe the Passover meal together. We read of this in Matthew 26. In verses 26-29, Jesus reveals this new way that His followers are to remember Him.

> *And as they were eating, Jesus took bread, blessed and broke it, and gave it to the disciples and said, "Take, eat; this is My body." Then He took the cup, and gave thanks, and gave it to them, saying, "Drink from it, all of you. For*

---

[66] See Romans 3:21-26.
[67] You can read of the Passover in Exodus 11-12.

> *this is My blood of the new covenant, which is shed for many for the remission of sins. But I say to you, I will not drink of this fruit of the vine from now on until that day when I drink it new with you in My Father's kingdom."*

This occurred at the end of the Passover celebration. Jesus was instituting a new supper that would replace his fulfillment of the imagery of the Passover. His death on the cross which would occur the next day was the final sacrifice for sin that provided deliverance from the judgment and slavery of sin for all mankind. Jewish Christians may have continued to celebrate Passover, but certainly they did it with a new understanding. You do not find New Testament Christians emphasizing the celebration of Passover but they did meet regularly to observe the Lord's Supper.

Instruction about the Lord's Supper

The Corinthians were guilty of many abuses in their observance of the Lord's Supper, so the apostle Paul gives a lengthy explanation and exhortation to the church at Corinth in 1 Corinthians 10:16-22 and 11:17-34. We can benefit greatly from studying these passages of the Scripture so that we might worship the Lord Jesus in a worthy manner as we come to His table. The Lord's Supper is a special time of worship for believers in Jesus Christ.

- **The meaning of the Lord's Supper**

The two basic elements of the Lord's Supper are the bread and the cup. Paul is rehearsing the words of Jesus as he explains the basic significance of the Lord's Supper. 1 Corinthians 11:23-26 says:

> *For I received from the Lord that which I also delivered to you: that the Lord Jesus on the same night in which He was betrayed took bread; and when He had given thanks, He broke it and said, "Take, eat; this is My body which is broken for you; do this in remembrance of Me." In the same manner He also took the cup after supper, saying, "This cup is the new covenant in My blood. This do, as often as you drink it, in remembrance of Me." For as often as you eat*

this bread and drink this cup, you proclaim the Lord's death till He comes.

- ## Commemoration of Christ's death on the cross

The bread is blessed and broken as a symbol of the body of Jesus that was broken on the cross as He bore the sin of the whole world upon Himself. The bread symbolizes your faith in the work of Christ on the cross where He absorbed God's judgment and wrath against your sin. By partaking of the bread, you are visually expressing your gratitude to Christ for taking your place - being your substitute on the cross.

The partaking of the bread is followed by drinking from the cup containing grape juice or, in some churches, wine. The grapes are crushed to produce the wine, symbolic of the bruising of Christ on the cross. The cup symbolizes the blood of Christ that was shed to cleanse you from all sin. It is through the shedding of Christ's blood for the sins of the world that you gained salvation as a free gift from God. As you drink of the cup, you give thanks from your heart for the shed blood of Christ that cleansed you and keeps on cleansing you from all sin.

- ## One way of proclaiming Christ's death

Verse 26 says, *"For as often as you eat this bread and drink this cup, you proclaim the Lord's death until He comes."* Your participation in the Lord's Supper is a way of proclaiming the gospel to others. By faithfully coming to the table of the Lord, you are boldly announcing your faith in Christ and His atoning work on the cross. Any non-believers who may be present will hear and see a presentation of the gospel of God's grace.

- ## Assurance of Christ's new covenant

Note Paul's words in verse 25 which he received from Christ Himself. *". . . This cup is the new covenant in My blood. This do, as often as you drink it, in remembrance of Me."* What is the new covenant? A covenant is an agreement or a promise that God has made with man.

The Lord Himself told us that the sign of the new covenant is the cup of the Lord's Supper.

God's covenant is a one-sided covenant for we are not in any position as sinners to bargain with God. He has made all the provision for our salvation through Christ, His sacrificial Lamb. He has also laid down all the conditions. He has said that we must come in repentance and place our trust in Christ Jesus as the One who has died in our place of the cross. If we will do this, trusting only in His shed blood to cleanse away our sin, He will forgive our sins and grant us eternal life as a free gift.

Some teach that baptism is the sign of the new covenant even as circumcision was the sign of the old covenant. This is not found in Scripture.

- **A regular reminder of Christ's second coming**

Every time you partake of the Lord's Supper, you are reminded that Jesus Christ has promised to come a second time to receive all of His followers to Himself. On the night that Jesus gave the Lord's Supper to His disciples, He said that He would not *"drink of this fruit of the vine until that day when I drink it new with you My Father's kingdom."* [68] It is most probable that Jesus was referring to the "marriage supper of the Lamb" that is described in Revelation 19:6-10. This will be the time when Jesus gathers His true church, the bride, to Himself in heaven. We will be united with Him and be in His actual presence forever.

Who should partake of the Lord's Supper?

It is obvious that Jesus instituted the Lord's Supper with His disciples. It was not intended for the general crowd of human beings or for those who were not His followers. Only true believers, those who have chosen to be His followers, are to come to the table of the Lord. To come to the table, without faith in Christ as Savior and Lord, is to act as a hypocrite.

Churches have different policies regarding the Lord's Supper. Some have close communion, meaning that only members of that church can partake, or only members of their particular denomination. Other churches have open communion which means that anyone can partake of the Lord's Supper without any restrictions.

---

[68] Matthew 26:29

The biblical pattern, as I see it, is a modified form of open communion. There are two restrictions that the Bible gives for partaking of the Lord's Supper. First, you must be a born again believer, having been made alive spiritually by the Holy Spirit, in response to your repentant faith in Christ. Secondly, you are to examine yourself to be certain that you are walking in fellowship with Christ, having confessed and forsaken all known sin in your life. We will study more on this subject in the next section of this chapter.

The age question often comes up in regards to children partaking of the Lord's Supper. While there is no specific Scripture that speaks to this, it is likely that the early church did not allow children to partake until they had passed the age of their Barmitzvah or Bah-mitzvah, the age at which the Jewish child came to accept adult responsibility. My advice to parents is that they are responsible to decide when their children can meaningfully partake without eating or drinking judgment to their souls.[69] It is better to have our children wait until they are more aware of the serious nature of the Lord's Supper than to err by having them partake too soon.

How should we prepare for the Lord's Supper?

The Lord's Supper is a serious service in the life of the church and the life of the believer. We are commanded by Christ to partake in remembrance of Him.

When Paul wrote the Corinthian church, he was strong in his words of correction for this erring body of believers. In 1 Corinthians 11:17, he says: *"Now in giving these instructions I do not praise you, since you come together not for the better but for the worse."* He chastises them for some issues that corrupted their worship of the Lord and made their observance of the Lord's Supper unacceptable. In fact, Paul bluntly says, in verse 20: *"Therefore when you come together in one place, it is not to eat the Lord's Supper."* In other words, he is saying, you may think you are eating the Lord's Supper, but your behavior is such that it negates the Lord's Supper.

1. They were allowing divisions or factions among them (Verse 18).

---

[69] Heed the Apostle Paul's warning in 1 Corinthians 11:27-30.

2. They were having a great feast and some were gluttonous and others were getting drunk. They were disregarding some members of the body by not waiting until all could come and eat together and worship the Lord through a proper observance of the Lord's Supper. In the early church, there were free citizens who could come and go as they pleased. There were also Christians who were slaves and they had their duties to perform before they could come to worship. These believing slaves would come and find that their free Christian brothers had already consumed the food without remembering the needs of the Christian slaves. As believers we are not only to remember Christ as we partake of the Lord's Supper, but we are to be conscious of the needs of our Christian brothers and sisters.

3. Paul also identifies some in the church whom he says are sick and others who have died because they have not partaken of the Lord's Supper in a worthy manner. Note that Paul is not speaking of being worthy to partake, for none of us is worthy in ourselves to come to the Lord's table. We are worthy to come to the table of the Lord Jesus only because we are made worthy through His cleansing us from our sin by His shed blood on the cross of Calvary. He is speaking about the manner in which they were partaking of the Lord's Supper. Note 1 Corinthians 11:27-32.

> *Therefore whoever eats this bread or drinks this cup of the Lord in an unworthy manner will be guilty of the body and blood of the Lord. But let a man examine himself, and so let him eat of the bread and drink of the cup. For he who eats and drinks in an unworthy manner eats and drinks judgment to himself, not discerning the Lord's body. For this reason many are weak and sick among you, and many sleep. For if we would judge ourselves, we would not be judged. But when we are judged, we are chastened by the Lord, that we may not be condemned with the world.*

Paul says that each believer has the responsibility to "*examine himself*" (Verse 28) and then partake of the Lord's Supper. How can a believer partake in a worthy manner if he is harboring some grudge against another person or is guilty of some other sin that he has not forsaken and confessed to the Lord? How can a believer come in a worthy manner if his heart is far from the Lord? How can a believer partake of the Lord's Supper in a worthy manner if his mind is preoccupied with the roast in the oven for Sunday dinner or the football game that he is missing on TV?

So prepare your heart and mind to worship the Lord and to give thanks to the Lord for His great sacrifice for you. Treat this special worship time as a great privilege afforded you by the Lord Jesus Himself.

How often are we to partake of the Lord's Supper?

Some churches partake of the Lord's Supper every week as they gather to worship the Lord. Some partake once a month; others only once every three months. The Bible does not speak to this question. Paul simply says, *"as often as you eat the bread and drink the cup. . ."* As I understand the Scriptures, the frequency of the Lord's Supper is not of crucial nature. What is important is that it is practiced in a worthy manner and for the right purpose.

It is a matter of the heart

A wife sits across the table from her husband as they are out for dinner on their anniversary. Instead of his attention and love being focused upon his wife, he sits reading the newspaper. She disgustingly says to her husband, "You don't care about me much do you, when you sit reading the newspaper on our date?" She is rightfully upset. How do you think Jesus Christ feels when we come to His table but our minds are focused on things other than Him?

Charles Haddon Spurgeon, one of the greatest preachers of the late 1800's, said this about Jesus Christ's death on the cross:

> "For his sin, man was condemned to eternal fire. When God took Christ to be the substitute, it is true that He did not send Christ into eternal fire. But He poured upon Him grief so desperate that it was a valid payment for even an eternity of fire. Man was condemned to live forever in hell. God did not send Christ forever into hell, but He placed on Christ a punishment that was equivalent for that. Although He did not give Christ to drink the actual hells of believers, yet He gave Him . . . something that was equivalent there unto. He

took the cup of Christ's agony, and He put in there suffering, misery, and anguish, such as only God can imagine or dream of. It was the exact equivalent of all the suffering, all the woe, and all the eternal tortures of everyone who shall at last stand in heaven, bought with the blood of Christ."

How is your heart when you come to the Lord's table? Is your heart divided? Is Christ Jesus the focus of your full attention, your love and thanksgiving? When you come to the table of the Lord, let it be to contemplate and give thanks for the great unimaginable suffering of Christ who died in your place that you might be forgiven and granted eternal life as a free gift. May your heart and mind worship Him who alone is worthy of your worship!

Some Study Questions for Your Reflection

1. What two biblical ordinances are commanded of believers in Jesus Christ?
2. What other terms are used to refer to the Lord's Supper?
3. What does a sacrament mean? Why do evangelical churches refer to baptism and the Lord's Supper as ordinances rather than sacraments?
4. What Old Testament feast was Jesus observing when He instituted what we now refer to as the Lord's Supper? What event did that Jewish feast celebrate?
5. What is the primary meaning of the bread and the cup?
6. How often does the New Testament teach us to observe the Lord's Supper?
7. What are some other meanings of the Lord's Supper?
8. What does it mean to partake of the Lord's Supper in an unworthy manner?
9. Paul speaks of the judgment of God that some of the Corinthian Christians experienced by partaking in an unworthy manner? How did God judge them?
10. How should you prepare to partake of the Lord's Supper? In what ways should you examine yourself?

Chapter 9

Holy Living In An Unholy World!

As Christians, we still live in this world but we are to live here as citizens of the kingdom of God, not citizens of this world. We are to live in the world without being conformed to the patterns of this world. A ship is to be in the water, in fact, cannot function unless it is in the water. However, the ship is in real trouble when water gets into the ship. In the same way, we Christians are to be in the world, without the world getting into us. We are not to isolate ourselves from the world as monks seek to do. Rather, we are to shine as lights in this world. We are to be salt and light in this world.[70]

Paul, the apostle, says in Romans 12:1-2:

> *I beseech you therefore, brethren, by the mercies of God, that you present your bodies a living sacrifice, holy, acceptable to God, which is your reasonable service. And do not be conformed to this world, but be transformed by the renewing of your mind, that you may prove what is that good and acceptable and perfect will of God.*

Our task as Christians is to live in this world without letting the world pressure us into its mold. We are to be continually being transformed by the power of the Holy Spirit renewing our minds. The word for "transformed" in verse 2 is translated from the root word from which we get our English word "metamorphous." Metamorphous is the process by which a caterpillar becomes a butterfly. We are in the process of becoming more and more like Jesus Christ.

As followers of Jesus Christ, our desire should be obedience to Jesus Christ in all our thoughts, our motives and our actions. The world in which we live is constantly exerting its pressure to have us go along with its evil deceptive ways. It takes strength from the Lord Jesus to stand against the pressure to conform.

---

70 See Matthew 5:13-16

God calls us to holy living

The primary attribute of God is His holiness. Throughout God's revelation of Himself in Scripture, it is obvious that God is holy in every aspect of His being. He is perfect in all His ways and is not tainted by any imperfection or flaw. In the very essence of His nature, God is holy. He is perfect in every respect.

The word 'holy' is often used in the Old Testament to speak of people and things that are dedicated exclusively to God. The priests were to set themselves to be 'holy' to God and all of the vessels and tools used in the tabernacle, and later in the temple, were 'holy' to God. This simply means that they were totally dedicated for God's use, for His purposes only. The people of Israel were to be holy to God. God rescued them as a nation out of slavery in Egypt and called them forth to be His holy people. Leviticus 11:44-45 says:

> *For I am the LORD your God. You shall therefore consecrate yourselves, and you shall be holy; for I am holy. Neither shall you defile yourselves with any creeping thing that creeps on the earth. For I am the LORD who brings you up out of the land of Egypt, to be your God. You shall therefore be holy, for I am holy.*

The apostle Peter is clearly quoting from this passage and others as he writes of God's call to holiness in 1 Peter 1:13-16.

> *Therefore gird up the loins of your mind, be sober, and rest your hope fully upon the grace that is to be brought to you at the revelation of Jesus Christ; as obedient children, not conforming yourselves to the former lusts, as in your ignorance; but as He who called you is holy, you also be holy in all your conduct, because it is written, "Be holy, for I am holy."*

The word "holy" in the New Testament Greek language is the word "hagios." When God commands that his redeemed people are to be holy, He means that we are to be set apart to God for His sacred purposes. This means that we are called to live in a pure, sinless and upright way that we might serve God's will only.

The apostle Paul says that the child of God is led by the Spirit of God. Romans 8:14 says: *"For as many as are led by the Spirit of*

God, these are the sons of God." As we study Romans 8:1-17, we will discover that the Spirit of God never leads believers to fulfill the desires of the old sinful nature. He always leads us to fulfill the desires of the Holy Spirit. Over the years, as a pastor, I have heard many professing Christians seek to justify their sinful actions by claiming that God was leading them. For example, one professing Christian man was a deacon in the church. He gave into his old fleshly desires and began a relationship with a woman other than his wife. He ended up divorcing his wife and marrying the other woman, claiming "we love each other so much, so this just has to be God's will." Do not be deceived; God never leads a person to do anything that is clearly contrary to Scripture, for the Holy Spirit never leads a person to violate God's commands.

How can I be holy before the Father?

The gospel tells us how we can be holy before God. We can never be declared holy before God through any effort of our own. We are justified, that is, we are "declared holy" before God only through the shed blood of Jesus Christ upon the cross. When we accepted Jesus Christ as our Savior, we transferred our trust to Him and His work of redemption on the cross. We ceased depending upon what we could do to make us right before God. We began trusting only in what God, the Son, has done for us in bearing our sin penalty on the cross.

From the time that we trusted Jesus Christ as our Savior from sin, we have been given a holy standing before the Father. Our sin is forgiven and cleansed away forever. We are not <u>made holy and righteous</u> in our entire daily walk as yet. That will happen on the day when we are home with the Lord in heaven. Here on this earth, we are works in progress. However, we are already <u>declared holy and righteous</u> (justified) on the basis of the holiness and righteousness of Jesus Christ, God's Son. Paul, the apostle, wrote of this in Romans 3:21-26:

> *But now the righteousness of God apart from the law is revealed, being witnessed by the Law and the Prophets, even the righteousness of God, through faith in Jesus Christ, to all and on all who believe. For there is no difference; for all have sinned and fall short of the glory of God, being justified freely by His grace through the redemption that is in Christ Jesus, whom God set forth as a propitiation by His blood, through faith, to demonstrate His righteousness,*

because in His forbearance God had passed over the sins that were previously committed, to demonstrate at the present time His righteousness, that He might be just and the justifier of the one who has faith in Jesus.

The transaction of declaring us holy and righteous before the Heavenly Father is a two-fold transaction. Holiness before God is first of all the absence of any sin or defilement. Every sin we have ever committed has been forgiven and washed away. Our record is cleared for eternity. However, holiness is also the presence of positive righteousness, not just the absence of sin and defilement. We are also declared righteous in God's sight in a positive sense because the success of doing God's complete will perfectly has been done for us by Jesus Christ Himself.

Suppose I owed a tremendous debt to my bank, a debt of ten million dollars. I defaulted and could not pay my debt. So I go to the bank to face the bad news and to be confronted by my creditors. As I arrive at the bank, the bank president meets me with a smile on his face. "You will not believe what just happened. Someone came in this morning and paid off your debt completely. You owe nothing!" As I am celebrating the good news, the banker says, "Oh, by the way, he not only paid off your debt. He also opened a savings account for you and deposited another ten million dollars." Then the celebration really begins. Not only has the debt been completely paid, but I am also rich.

That is, in essence, what has happened for every believer in Jesus Christ. The debt we owed is completely wiped out. Besides that, God, the Father views us in the same righteous and holy way that He views His Son, Jesus Christ. We are declared free from sin and completely righteous before God.

As we live out our pilgrimage on this earth, we are to live in a righteous and holy way because of what Christ has done for us. We are called to live out holy lives, but not as an effort to become righteous before God. We already have that righteous standing before God through faith. Now we are to live holy lives so that our every-day lives will match up to our standing that we have been given as a free gift. As the apostle, Paul, wrote in Titus 2:11-14:

For the grace of God that brings salvation has appeared to all men, teaching us that, denying ungodliness and worldly lusts, we should live soberly, righteously, and godly in the present age, looking for the blessed hope and glorious appearing of our great God and Savior Jesus Christ, who gave Himself for us, that He might redeem us from every lawless deed and purify for Himself His own special people, zealous for good works.

A culture morally adrift

The United States was founded upon a common belief in the God of the Bible. With this foundational belief, there was a commitment to the existence of absolute truth even though many did not hold to a personal saving faith in Jesus Christ. In World War II days, there was still a considerable commitment to absolute truth even upon the part of non-Christians. It was commonly accepted that there was an objective standard for truth outside of our human selves. Truth was anchored in God.

In the 1960's and the 1970's, a public moral rebellion began when the "hippie" generation threw away moral restraints. "Free love" and the drug culture emerged. Such behavior sought a belief system that would reduce the guilt feelings. So liberal theologians, like Joseph Fletcher, began to speak of the death of God and they taught a relative morality. Nothing was absolutely right or absolutely wrong - it all depended upon the circumstances. Timothy O'Leary developed a rationale for the drug culture and encouraged a whole generation "to space out" as a way to "really live."

A continuing erosion of moral and ethical absolutes has progressed to the point where our secular educational system in America has accepted the axiom that "there is no such thing as absolute truth." Secular educators teach this with straight face, seemingly not recognizing that they have just stated an absolute. Our children and our youth are being taught that each person must decide for himself what his truth is. They are also being taught that they must never make any judgment about anyone else's life style, because he or she has his or her "own truth" that works for them. In other words, America's universities and public schools now teach a "designer truth." Every person designs his own truth that works for him. Therefore no one's truth can claim any ascendancy over any other person's truth. This is Satan's lie that is steadily leading America to disaster.

Charles Colson writes:

"You see, in the past, non-Christians rejected the Bible as true, but today many of them reject any notion of truth at all. American society has split into two groups. On one side are those who accept the idea of an objective truth - and yes, "true values." On the other side are those who believe truth and values are relative and subjective.

The split between these two groups is so severe that some sociologists are calling it a culture war. It is a rift that imperils our very existence as a nation.

Every political order must rest on a moral order, a shared set of beliefs and values. What binds society together is the trust that we will all regulate our conduct according to some agreed-upon moral framework.

But since the 1960's, the very notion of a common moral framework has steadily eroded. Today many people believe that we can set our own standards - that ethics is just a matter of individual feelings and choices." [71]

This is the world in which we live. Our world is very similar to the world of the first century church. Moral relativism was rampant then also. Those who followed Jesus Christ and claimed that He was God were a minority as they stood for the One True God and His absolute truth, often at the risk of their lives.

The world's way versus God's way

In 1 John 2:15-17, we read this exhortation:

> *Do not love the world or the things in the world. If anyone loves the world, the love of the Father is not in him. For all that is in the world, the lust of the flesh, the lust of the eyes, and the pride of life, is not of the Father but is of the world. And the world is passing away, and the lust of it; but he who does the will of God abides forever.*

The world system is opposed to the kingdom of God. The world system is based upon the old sinful nature. The things of the

---

[71] Charles Colson, A Dance With Deception (Word Books, Dallas, Texas, 1993) p. 19.

world appeal to the old sinful nature through the lustful desires of our physical drives, through what we see with our eyes and long to have. The world system teaches that we are the masters of our fate leading us to the pride and boasting of what we possess and what we have achieved in this temporal life. Therefore the Lord commands us as believers to stop loving the world and the things in this world.

James 4:4 poses a choice to the follower of Christ.

> *". . . Do you not know that friendship with the world is enmity with God? Whoever therefore wants to be a friend of the world makes himself an enemy of God."*

We cannot be fence sitters. Either we determine to be friends and followers of Christ or friends and followers of the world system.

This is what Jesus said to His disciples and He still says the same to us:

> *If the world hates you, you know that it hated Me before it hated you. If you were of the world, the world would love its own. Yet because you are not of the world, but I chose you out of the world, therefore the world hates you. Remember the word that I said to you, 'A servant is not greater than his master.' If they persecuted Me, they will also persecute you. If they kept My word, they will keep yours also.* (John 15:18-20).

God's absolutes

The truth is that Jehovah God alone is God and that He is Sovereign over all things that exist. His "Sovereignty" means that God rules over all things. All things were created by God and without Him nothing exists. God is Sovereign by the right of creation and He is also Sovereign by the right of redemption. With the rightful authority as Sovereign God, God has established His absolute truth.

The word of God, the Bible, is God's revelation to us of Himself and His plan. Therefore when God speaks through His Word, His Word stands as absolute truth. His Word will never fail and it does not change as our culture changes.

In many places in His Word God clearly forbids things as being absolutely wrong. These behaviors by mankind are always sinful and bring His judgment. For example, the Ten Commandments found in Exodus 20:1-17 are absolute truth. When God says "You shall not commit adultery," He means it for all time and for all circumstances. No situation in which you find yourself justifies committing adultery. When He says "You shall not steal," He does not mean that it is all right to steal from your employer if you are not making enough money in your job.

Some of His absolutes are positive commands that we are not to leave undone. If we omit these positive absolutes, we also are committing sin. James 4:17 says: *"Therefore, to him who knows to do good, and does not do it, to him it is sin."* God commands us to love each other and we are also to love our enemies. These are absolutes and are non-negotiable.

Beware that, as a Christian, you are not deceived by the world's definitions and philosophies that rationalize sinful behavior. Measure everything by God's Word.

Some areas of our lives: it all depends!

But what if God's Word doesn't say anything about a decision we are facing? Such issues do not fall into the category of God's absolutes. In fact, there are some things that may be right for one believer and wrong for another. It all depends upon what is God's best for our lives.

The apostle Paul speaks about this in 1 Corinthians 6:12 where he says *"All things are lawful for me, but all things are not helpful. All things are lawful for me, but I will not be brought under the power of any."* Is Paul saying that even adultery was lawful for him? Obviously not, for in the context of this chapter, he has already made it clear that sexual immorality is sinful. So is sex always sinful and forbidden by God? No! Within the marriage relationship sex is holy and pure, but outside of marriage, it is forbidden and sinful. So the marriage relationship determines whether or not sex is holy and proper.

But what do we do about life style issues that cannot be answered with a verse from the Bible? We will need to seek God's will through prayer and careful application of the principles of God's Word. When we seek to make a decision about whom we should marry, how will we decide what is the Lord's will? When we are faced with a decision about whether or not we should buy a new automobile, how will we decide the Lord's will? We will face situations almost every day of our lives when we will not be able to point to a specific verse of Scripture to determine God's will.

One of the situations that confronted the first century Christians was whether or not to eat meat that had been offered to idols. They lived in an idolatrous culture where meat that was sold in the markets was often first offered in sacrifice to the gods in the temples. New Christians, who used to be idol worshipers, were often plagued in their consciences when they partook of such meat. Paul saw all meat as created by God and the offering of it to an idol did not affect his strong conscience. It was perfectly lawful for him to eat it but for the sake of the conscience of a weaker brother, he would not eat meat if it would be an offense to his brother (1 Corinthians 8:13).

Legalism: a man-made code of conduct

I grew up in a fine gospel-preaching, Bible believing church in western Canada. It was much like many other evangelical churches. The people had good hearts and desired to follow Christ obediently. As a teen-ager, I soon learned that certain things were not to be done and certain places were out of bounds for a Christian. Sometimes we look back remembering that we were not to "smoke, drink or chew and we were not go with girls who do." There were about a dozen rules by which we were to abide, all of which were negative rules. If we managed to avoid breaking this set of rules, we were regarded as "good Christians."

This we call legalism. It is the trap into which the biblical Pharisees had fallen. They had established a code of conduct for God's people, seeking to establish a rule for every conceivable circumstance a person might face. Like the Pharisees, we also can fall into the erroneous belief that sees spirituality as refraining from certain behaviors. Managing to obey a set of man-imposed rules of conduct does not make a person spiritual. Spirituality is a love relationship with Jesus Christ that is guided by His Holy Spirit.

Legalism overlooks more important matters of the heart. The Christian who doesn't drink alcoholic beverages may excuse his gossip. The Christian who has never smoked, or who has gained victory over this bad habit, may excuse his overeating. When we refuse to accept a legalistic code of conduct, it does not mean that we ought to go out and engage in those negative behaviors. It does mean that there is a better way. We are to be guided by the Spirit of God through the Word of God.

One of the results of legalism is that one becomes proud of his success in keeping the rules and he becomes blind to more subtle areas of sin in his life. Paul describes this problem when he writes to the church of Colossae. Colossians 2:20-23 says:

> *Therefore, if you died with Christ from the basic principles of the world, why, as though living in the world, do you subject yourselves to regulations - "Do not touch, do not taste, do not handle," which all concern things which perish with the using - according to the commandments and doctrines of men? These things indeed have an appearance of wisdom in self-imposed religion, false humility, and neglect of the body, but are of no value against the indulgence of the flesh.*

Legalism leads to judging your brother

The apostle Paul addresses the matter of "doubtful things" in Romans 14. As you read this chapter, you will find Paul talks about "weak" and "strong" Christians. The strong Christian is the one who has a lot of freedom in his conscience and he could tend to "look down" on the weaker Christian who has not yet developed freedom of conscience through his growth in the Word of God. The weak Christian is the one who is restricted in his freedom because many things bother him and he has a tendency to judge the stronger Christian who exercises his freedom. Romans 14:1-6 reads:

> *Receive one who is weak in the faith, but not to disputes over doubtful things. For one believes he may eat all things, but he who is weak eats only vegetables. Let not him who eats despise him who does not eat, and let not him who does not eat judge him who eats; for God has received him. Who are you to judge another's servant? To his own master he stands or falls. Indeed, he will be made to stand, for God is able to make him stand.*
>
> *One person esteems one day above another; another esteems every day alike. Let each be fully convinced in his*

own mind. He who observes the day, observes it to the Lord; and he who does not observe the day, to the Lord he does not observe it. He who eats, eats to the Lord, for he gives God thanks; and he who does not eat, to the Lord he does not eat, and gives God thanks.

Note that Paul is not speaking about the absolutes which God has laid out in His Word. He is speaking about observance of special days. Some believed that one day a week was to be observed as a total day of rest and worship. Others sensed more freedom and believed that every day was a day to serve the Lord. Paul speaks also about dietary matters. No doubt he has in mind the situation that he addressed in 1 Corinthians 8 when he spoke of the Christian's attitude in partaking of meat offered to idols. Some wouldn't touch such meat in any way and so had chosen to eat only vegetables. Others had freedom of conscience, like Paul, and viewed the meat as created by God to enjoy.

Legalists, who have their code of conduct, do tend not to hold their convictions only between themselves and God, but they often impose their code on all other believers. They also tend to judge and reprimand their brothers who do not abide by their self-imposed code.

On the other hand, strong Christians who are free in their consciences run the risk of becoming libertines. Their freedom can be used to indulge the old sinful nature if they are not careful in their walk with the Lord. Paul warns us in Galatians 5:13-14:

For you, brethren, have been called to liberty; only do not use liberty as an opportunity for the flesh, but through love serve one another. For all the law is fulfilled in one word, even in this: "You shall love your neighbor as yourself."

The tendency to use one's liberty as an opportunity for the flesh is countered by living a life of love toward others. In considering your brother lovingly, you will be careful not to offend your weaker brother.

Biblical principles by which the Holy Spirit guides

So how do we follow the Holy Spirit's guidance as we make decisions about the "doubtful things"?

There are a number of principles taught in Scripture that Paul outlines in Romans 14 and 1 Corinthians 6. As we seek to be guided by the Holy Spirit in applying these principles, we will please the Lord in our living.

- **Anything that harms the body is sin**

Paul teaches that the body of the Christian is the temple of the Holy Spirit and he is to use his body in holy ways. 1 Corinthians 6:19-20 says:

> *. . . do you not know that your body is the temple of the Holy Spirit who is in you, whom you have from God, and you are not your own? For you were bought at a price; therefore glorify God in your body and in your spirit, which are God's.*

In the context Paul is speaking about using the body for illicit sex. Can you even begin to think about taking your body that belongs to Christ and link it up with a harlot?

The same principle applies to other harmful behaviors that are damaging to the body. When you apply the principle instead of adopting a code of conduct, you do not overlook any harmful behavior. So you do not apply the principle simply in the case of smoking or drinking alcohol but you see that the principle applies equally when it comes to overeating or not getting proper rest and exercise.

As you are seeking to walk by the Spirit, ask yourself this question: "Does what I am doing, or contemplating doing, harm my body and contaminate the temple of God's Holy Spirit?"

- **Anything that causes a brother to stumble is sin**

Paul instructs in Romans 14:12-13: *"So then each of us shall give account of himself to God. Therefore let us not judge one another anymore, but rather resolve this, not to put a stumbling block or a cause to fall in our brother's way."* Every Christian is to be watching out for the best interest of his brothers and sisters in Christ.

For example, if a new believer is a former alcoholic, he may be caused to stumble back into his old way if he sees me have a glass of wine with my meal. This is one of the major reasons that I have chosen to be a total abstainer from drinking alcoholic beverages. (Besides this, my father taught me that being an abstainer is the safe way to life. I will never risk becoming an alcoholic if I never partake of alcoholic drinks). I am also convinced that it is the best example to set for my children and grandchildren. It would devastate me if I would cause any of them to stumble over my poor example. John MacArthur Jr. comments:

> "The same principle applies to any activity or practice that is not inherently sinful. Problem areas vary from society to society and from person to person, but the principle never changes. The loving, caring, strong Christian will determine in his mind and heart to be sensitive to any weakness in a fellow believer and avoid doing anything, including what is innocent in itself and otherwise permissible, that might cause him to morally or spiritually stumble." [72]

During World War II, when vessels had to be convoyed across the Atlantic because of the U-boat menace, all vessels had to adjust their speed to that of the slowest. This is the idea Paul is driving home here. Sure, the stronger brother could stride ahead, but love will not permit it. The shepherd must pace the flock to accommodate the weakest lamb. The Christian must regulate his freedom to take into consideration the feeble conscience of the weakest.[73]

In Romans 14:15-18, Paul teaches us that we are showing love to our brothers by such restrained living. When we care for our brothers enough to abstain from something we can do with a clear conscience, in order to help them avoid stumbling into sin, we are "serving Christ" in an acceptable way.[74] The strong

---

[72] John MacArthur Jr., Romans 9-16 Commentary (Moody Press, Chicago, IL, 1994) p. 291.
[73] John Phillips, Exploring Romans (Moody Press, Chicago, IL, 1969) pp 241f.
[74] For further study of this subject, see Romans 14:20-21 and 1 Corinthians 8:1-13. The early church problem was meat offered to idols and then served in idol temple restaurants or sold in meat markets for home consumption.

Christian, mature in his faith and freedom, will limit his freedom in order to show love to a weaker brother.

- **Anything that does not build up yourself or others is sin**

As Christians we are to be in the building business instead of the wrecking business. We are to be concerned about edifying or building up ourselves and others in the faith and in Christ-like living. Paul tells us, in Romans 14:19: *"Therefore let us pursue the things which make for peace and the things by which one may edify another."*

When we give ourselves to helping others to grow in the Lord, we find that we are also growing in the Lord. President John F. Kennedy inspired the nation when he said, "Ask not what your country can do for you, but what can you do for your country." What a great motto for us as Christians: "Ask not what your church or others can do for you, but ask what you can do for your church and for others."

We are to "pursue the things that make for peace" and things that encourage others to grow in grace and knowledge of our Lord. Be a builder, not a wrecker!

- **Anything that enslaves you and becomes your master is sin**

All people come to Christ out of a background of slavery. We are enslaved to sinful habits of various kinds. Some are enslaved to alcohol, drugs or smoking. Others are enslaved to sex and many have adopted pornography as a lifestyle. Still others are enslaved to material things, and possessing more and more of this world's goods is an obsession. Some are enslaved to food. They live to eat rather than eat to live. Others are enslaved to sports and entertainment. Television rules the lives of many people. It is impossible to list all the masters to which people are enslaved.

The world's philosophy is "if it feels good, do it!" For Christians, this cannot be our motto. We are redeemed from sin and are not to continue on in our old sinful ways. We are to live in our freedom in Christ Jesus.

In 1 Corinthians 6:12, Paul says,

> *"All things are lawful for me, but all things are not helpful. All things are lawful for me, but I will not be brought under the power of any."*

Whenever we are addicted to anything as our master, we are sinning. As born again Christians, we have been given the Holy Spirit to free us from the grip and power of sin. When Jesus sets us free, we are free indeed![75]

As Christians, we acknowledge Jesus Christ as our Master and our Lord. He has set us free so that we are no longer obligated to obey sin as our master. Read and study Romans 6. You will see that we are now free from our sin master. We are free to choose to serve our new Master, Jesus Christ. Before we trusted Christ as Savior, we were not free. We were chained to Satan and to our old sin nature. Our old nature controlled us and mastered us. But now we are freed by Christ to choose to serve Him and to give our bodies as living sacrifices to do what is right in God's sight. Dr. Warren Wiersbe writes:

> "Jesus Christ bought us with a price (1 Corinthians 6:20), and therefore our bodies belong to Him. We are one spirit with the Lord and we must yield our bodies to Him as living sacrifices (Romans 12:1-2). If you begin each day by surrendering your body to Christ, it will make a great deal of difference in what you do with your body during the day."[76]

As Christians, the Lord wants us to live in freedom. We must evaluate our lives in regards to slavery. Is there something that is still holding us in its grip? Confess it to the Lord as sin and find moment by moment freedom in your relationship with Jesus Christ who frees us from the slavery of sin.

Victory is gained in Christ Jesus when we focus upon our love relationship with Jesus Christ, our new Master and Savior. When we focus upon the enslaving sin and seek to just quit doing it in our own strength, we will usually set ourselves up for failure.

---

[75]   See John 8:36
[76]   Warren Wiersbe, Be Wise, 1 Corinthians (Victor Books, Wheaton, IL, 1988) p. 72.

When we get to know Jesus Christ in an intimate way through the Word of God and prayer, we will love Him more and more. We will find that our love for God and our desire to please Him will enable us to trust Him for His power to resist the devil and to resist the temptation of our enslaving habits. Our desire to please Him will be greater than our desire for the temporary pleasure provided by our sinful enslaving habit.

- **Anything that your conscience forbids is sin**

God has given each of us a conscience. The conscience is that inner part of us that is designed to guide us to proper conduct. The conscience is molded to some extent by our upbringing in our childhood and by all the influences around us. The conscience may be uninformed and create unnecessary guilt because of negative influences and negative training in our lives. For example, if you have had negative parents, who were always labeling you as a sinner because you were not abiding by their self imposed rules of righteousness, you may have guilt feelings over the most harmless things. As a ridiculous example, if you have been told all your growing-up-years that eating potatoes is sinful, you will feel guilty every time you eat potatoes, until your mind is enlightened by the truth that potatoes are good for you.

Paul tells us that we are to obey our consciences until such time as our consciences are enlightened by proper knowledge and we are freed in our consciences. Note that Paul is dealing with this matter of a "weak" or a "strong" conscience in 1 Corinthians 8:4-7.

> *Therefore concerning the eating of things offered to idols, we know that an idol is nothing in the world, and that there is no other God but one. For even if there are so-called gods, whether in heaven or on earth (as there are many gods and many lords), yet for us there is one God, the Father, of whom are all things, and we for Him; and one Lord Jesus Christ, through whom are all things, and through whom we live. However, there is not in everyone that knowledge; for some, with consciousness of the idol, until now eat it as a thing offered to an idol; and their conscience, being weak, is defiled.*

Proper knowledge is necessary for the conscience to work properly. Therefore we need to be continually feeding our minds on God's truth in order to have a spiritually mature and strong liberated conscience. Until such time that your conscience is biblically informed, you have a "weak" conscience. Even so, you are not to violate your conscience by doing something that your conscience forbids you to do. This is what Paul means when he writes in Romans 14:22-23:

> *Do you have faith? Have it to yourself before God. Happy is he who does not condemn himself in what he approves. But he who doubts is condemned if he eats, because he does not eat from faith; for whatever is not from faith is sin.*

When Paul asks about whether or not you have faith, he is asking about how you feel about any specific activity in which you are engaging. In other words, is your conscience free? Do you have faith or confidence that you are doing right in God's eyes? In regards to these doubtful areas of conduct, keep your faith or your convictions between you and God. Do not try to impose your convictions in the area of "doubtful things" upon other Christians. If your conscience is not free in regards to an activity that you decide to do, you are violating your conscience. You are not to do this activity because your conscience will condemn you and you will feel guilty. This means that you may not be able to do something that other Christians seem to be totally free to do because you cannot do it with a free and clear conscience before God.

- **Anything that does not bring glory to God is sin**

There is an over-arching principle that guides us in our decisions and our life activities. God has redeemed us and given His Holy Spirit to us. Christ Jesus is our life and He is resident and president of our lives. Paul sums up this truth in 1 Corinthians 10:31-33:

> *Therefore, whether you eat or drink, or whatever you do, do all to the glory of God. Give no offense, either to the Jews or to the Greeks or to the church of God, just as I also please all men in all things, not seeking my own profit, but the profit of many, that they may be saved.*

Some study questions for your reflection

1. What does it mean to "present your body" to God as a living sacrifice (Romans 12:1)? How can we do this as Christians?
2. What are some of the influences of the 'world system' that pressure us to conform to what everyone else is doing? When John says "Love not the world", what does he mean by the "world"? 1 John 2:15-17.
3. How can we as Christians resist this pressure to conform? As a Christian, how can you be transformed or changed?
4. What reason does Peter give for you to be holy? 1 Peter 1:15-16.
5. When we think about God as "holy," what does this mean? With some other words, describe God's holiness.
6. How does God give us a "holy standing" before Him? What is the relationship between our 'holy standing' before God and our call to live a godly, holy life?
7. Is there such a thing as 'absolute truth'? Where do we find absolute truth? Give some examples of absolute truths that come from God.
8. What is legalism? To what does legalism lead us?
9. What are some of the principles of Scripture by which we can make Spirit led decisions about "doubtful things"?
10. What is our responsibility toward a Christian whose conscience is still weak? What principles apply in our consideration of the weaker brother?
11. What is the key to finding victory over enslaving sinful habits?
12. What is the most important over-arching principle in our lives as Christians? 1 Corinthians 10:31.

Chapter 10

If God Loves Me, Why Does He Allow Me To Suffer?

Facing the Reality of Suffering

As a new believer, you soon find out that God has not promised you a rose garden. Knowing Christ personally as your Savior and knowing that your eternal destiny is secure is wonderful. However, you still find that weeds grow in your garden and you are not exempt from trouble.

It is not simply the aggravation of colds that disrupt your health, but Christians still get cancer and face losing their jobs and experiencing financial crises. Why?

It is an enigma to you when you find that the more you seek to follow the Lord Jesus, the more you seem to face the ridicule and the scoffing of the ungodly. When you seek to do what is right in God's eyes, you often are misunderstood. As the apostle Peter wrote in 1 Peter 3, Christians often suffer for doing right, but adds *"For it is better, if it is the will of God, to suffer for doing good than for doing evil"* (1 Peter 3:17).

Really, can it be God's will that we suffer for doing good? Yes, according to Peter. This is a subject that you will grapple with all of your Christian life and never completely understand and grasp. It becomes a matter of walking by faith and trusting God's Word when you cannot understand His reason for your suffering.

God's solid rock promise

There is a promise that Christians down through the centuries have held onto when they have gone through trial upon trial. The apostle Paul wrote to the church at Rome when the Christians were under persecution for no other reason than their faith in the Supreme Almighty God and their loyal trust in Jesus Christ alone. Romans 8:28 says *"And we know that all things work together for good to those who love God, to those who are the called according to His purpose."*

Do all things really work for our good and God's glory?

Some real life situations

On a pleasant Saturday close to Easter, in 1999, a young pastor, Ned Reish, of Chardon, Ohio, took his family to enjoy some plane rides with a friend he had met just a few days before. The man was a seasoned pilot who wanted to treat his new friends to their first plane rides. All the children and Vicki, Ned's wife, had completed their flights. Then it was Dad's turn. To the horror of all the rest who looked on, the plane never made it above some trees on take-off. It crashed, killing the pilot and this wonderful young pastor; and leaving Vicki as a widow and five children without a father.

A young couple had been married for a couple of years. They were believers who had committed themselves to Christ Jesus and sought to glorify God in their lives and in their marriage. They were both overjoyed to learn that the young lady was soon expecting the birth of their first child. On the day of the baby's arrival, their dreams were shattered when they learned from her attending doctor that their new-born son was born Downs-syndrome and would never be normal in his developmental growth.

Do bad things happen to God's redeemed people? Obviously, they do! As a matter of fact, each of us is able to share a story of personal tragedy either in his own life or in the life of a close friend. We all experience bad things over the course of our lives.

Yet we hear the words of Paul to the church at Rome as we find them in Romans 8:28:

> *And we know that in all things God works for the good of those who love him, who have been called according to his purpose.*

How do we reconcile this promise of God with the circumstances of our lives? Is this really true? Intellectually we may know that it is true because it is in the Bible. But in our emotions and in the trauma of every day experiences, it doesn't seem that way. We need to grapple with this seeming discrepancy between our experiences and the obvious stated truth of God's Word if we are to maintain our trust in the Lord our God.

R.C. Sproul states it in this way:

"In theory, it is easy to understand the premise that all things work together for good to those who love God and are called according to his purpose, but to get this into our bloodstreams is another matter. It is one of the most difficult tasks of the practicing Christian. It involves not only believing in God but believing God."[77]

Understand what God's promise does not say

As we grapple with the truth of God's Word, we must be certain that we are not misstating or misunderstanding what God says.

God does not say that all things that happen are good! Rather God promises that He will work all things together for our good and for His glory. He will dynamically work in all circumstances for our good, even in those happenings in life that seem to be so awful or so evil.

Paul, the apostle, qualifies this statement. He is speaking of true believers. This is not some blanket promise to be claimed by all people. It is God's promise to all who are trusting Christ as our Savior and Lord. You are an object of His special love and care.

This becomes a matter of faith, of every day, moment by moment trust. When your body or the body of a dear loved one is wracked with disease and pain; when you suffer the loss of your job; when you are being persecuted because you are a Christian; or you are experiencing some other bad thing, how do you trust God that He is working all things together for your good?

Trust in the good Person of God

When bad things happen to you as a Christian, Satan will immediately begin tempting you to blame God, to view God as your adversary. One of Satan's primary tactics is to malign the character of God. From the beginning of time Satan has sought to cast doubt in the minds of human beings as to God's character. Did he not use this tactic as he tempted Eve in the Garden of Eden? (Genesis 2:15-17). Ponder Satan's tactics as we read of them in Genesis 3:1-5:

---

[77] R. C. Sproul, The Invisible Hand, Do All Things Really Work For Good? (Word Publishing, Dallas, 1996) p 174

> *Now the serpent was more cunning than any beast of the field which the LORD God had made. And he said to the woman, "Has God indeed said, 'You shall not eat of every tree of the garden'?" And the woman said to the serpent, "We may eat the fruit of the trees of the garden; but of the fruit of the tree which is in the midst of the garden, God has said, 'You shall not eat it, nor shall you touch it, lest you die.'"*
>
> *Then the serpent said to the woman, "You will not surely die. For God knows that in the day you eat of it your eyes will be opened, and you will be like God, knowing good and evil."*

Satan casts doubt into Eve's mind about God's goodness. "*Has God indeed said . . .?*" Then he convinces her that God really is keeping her from being all that she could be. In my interpretative free translation, Satan says, "After all, God knows that in the day that you eat, you will then really know everything, in fact you will become just like God." In essence Satan wishes to convince us that God is really selfish in His command and He seeks to have us believe that which is not true of God.

The book of Job is considered by many scholars to be the oldest biblical book. It is the account of the great sufferer, Job, whom God tested in very severe ways. As you read the first chapter, you are confronted with a godly man who was *"blameless and upright and one who feared God and shunned evil."*[78] Job was a man who was greatly favored by God, who had a family of ten children and possessed great wealth.

Satan makes the accusation to God that Job is serving Him and fearing Him only because it paid financial dividends to do so. So Satan is given permission by God to attack Job in severe but limited ways. Satan could do as he wished with Job's children and his possessions but he was not allowed to attack his person. Job lost all of his children in tragic deaths and all of his possessions were quickly taken from him. We read this remarkable testimony in Job 1:22: *"In all this Job did not sin nor charge God with wrong."*

In chapter two, we find Satan doesn't give up easily. Before God Satan accuses Job of only serving God because a man will do anything for his own life. "Let me attack his health and he will

---

[78]   Job 1:1

curse you to your face, God!"[79] So Satan is given permission to do so. Job is afflicted with severe boils from the crown of his head to the souls of his feet. He is in utter misery. We read in Job 2:9-10 of his wife's response to her husband's suffering.

> *Then his wife said to him, "Do you still hold fast to your integrity? Curse God and die!" But he said to her, "You speak as one of the foolish women speaks. Shall we indeed accept good from God, and shall we not accept adversity?" In all this Job did not sin with his lips.*

Here is the testimony of a godly man of faith who refused to accuse God of evil and refused Satan's attempts to have him malign the character of God. And this is the first issue you must deal with when you are experiencing bad things in your life. You must come to grips with who God really is. Is He the good God that is revealed in Scripture, or is He the God that Satan is slandering as a God who is evil and does bad things to people just to be nasty?

What do the Scriptures say about God's good character? Here are only a few Bible verses to ponder.

> Psalms 73:1 says, *"Truly God is good to Israel, to such as are pure in heart."*

> Exodus 33:19: *"Then He said, 'I will make all My goodness pass before you, and I will proclaim the name of the LORD before you. I will be gracious to whom I will be gracious, and I will have compassion on whom I will have compassion.'"*

> Psalms 27:13: *"I would have lost heart, unless I had believed that I would see the goodness of the LORD In the land of the living."*

> Psalms 31:19: *"Oh, how great is Your goodness, which You have laid up for those who fear You, which You have prepared for those who trust in You in the presence of the sons of men!"*

---

79 Job 2:4-5 (The author's free translation)

In the context of the eighth chapter of Romans the apostle Paul emphasizes the goodness of God.

In v. 31, he says that "God is for us . . . not against us." He points out that God demonstrates his goodness by not sparing even His own Son, and if He did that, will He not graciously give us all things (Verse 32)? God chose us and justified us, that is, He declared us righteous through Christ and His shed blood.(Verse 33). He is the good God who will never allow us to be separated from His love (Verses 35-39).

So in the tragedies of life, who are you going to believe? Will you choose to believe God who is intrinsically good in His character, or Satan who maligns God's character? This is not just a matter of trusting in Him, but believing God's testimony about Himself, and basing your trust on the good character of God. As the Psalmist says in Psalms 34:8: *"Taste and see that the LORD is good; blessed is the man who takes refuge in him."*

Sometimes it is difficult for us to see "the goodness of God" in the midst of our pain. Joseph Stowell commented:

> "Comfort is not always good and goodness is not always comfortable. God never promised us a life of "birth-to-death" comfort. God may not always be comfortable, but He is always good." [80]

When bad things are happening to you and you can't understand God's ways, you need to be able to trust the fact that God is good. I remember some of the words of an anthem that our church choir has sung from time to time. "God is too wise to be mistaken. God is too good to be unkind. So when you don't understand, when you can't trace His hand, trust His heart!" [81]

Trust in the good purpose of God

According to Scripture, God's purpose or design for believers is always a good purpose. Paul emphasizes this in the last part of Romans 8:28 where he says *"God works for the good of those who love him, who have been called according to his purpose."* Verse 29 further clarifies that purpose. *"For those God foreknew he also*

---

80   Joseph Stowell, Through The Fire, (Victor Books, Wheaton, Illinois, 1985) p 35
81   From words of a song by Babbie Mason.

predestined to be conformed to the likeness of his Son, that he might be the firstborn among many brothers."

God is not silent in the Scriptures about His purpose in pain and difficulties. We do not find His difficult ways pleasant at times but it is not with a malicious purpose that God allows the troubles that come to our lives. Read what Paul writes in this same epistle to the church at Rome in Romans 5:3-4:

> *And not only that, but we also glory in tribulations, knowing that tribulation produces perseverance; and perseverance, character; and character, hope.*

In James 1:2-4 we find a command that is preposterous apart from faith in God's purpose for our suffering and testing.

> *My brethren, count it all joy when you fall into various trials, knowing that the testing of your faith produces patience. But let patience have its perfect work, that you may be perfect and complete, lacking nothing.*

Purpose always makes a difference in your outlook toward what is happening in your life. A person goes through surgery, trusting a doctor to cut him open, enduring all the pain, because of a good purpose. Have you noted the difference that purpose makes for kids getting out of bed in the morning - whether they are going to school or to the Six Flags Amusement Park?

I want to be sensitive to your feelings because you may be going through a severe trial right now, and you are feeling great pain. It is easy to quote Romans 8:28 as a casual verbal panacea for everyone who is going through pain.

Dr. Joseph Stowell tells of receiving the following letter after he had preached on the text of Romans 8:28.

> "Dear Pastor Stowell:
>
> I've thought of communicating with you on your current sermon theme (Romans 8:28). Since August 30, 1979, every time that theme comes up, I am painfully reminded of my brother's death by suicide.

> He left a widow with two small daughters. I had to identify him for the coroner and tell my parents what had happened. Then I had to clean the walls and ceilings and furniture of his blood and flesh, as he had shot himself in the head. The legacy of his death confronts us on a regular basis.
>
> I have asked myself often - what good was there in his death - to us - or to him? There is no answer.
>
> Except for a handful of close friends, the local church was not much comfort. Most acted as though it never happened." [82]

Even though I risk seeming to be insensitive to your pain right now, it is important that you trust the good purpose of God. So hang on to the truth that you know even though your feelings say otherwise. It is especially important because your feelings are fragile when you are going through the valley of suffering.

Dr. Stowell describes our feelings so well when we are going through troubled times. He writes:

> "Trouble brings with it a whole bucketful of emotions. Despair, hurt, revenge, self-pity, anger, sorrow and a dozen other feelings. If we are not careful, these feelings will dominate and disorient us from what we know. Emotions redirect our thoughts and detour our commitments. We tend to distort what we know by how we feel." [83]

A couple of years ago John Kennedy Junior, along with his wife and sister-in-law, were all tragically killed in the crash of his small plane. The most probable cause was pilot disorientation at night. A pilot can lose his orientation when flying in darkness or in clouds. At such a time, he must depend on his instruments instead of his feelings. He can be flying in a circle or rapidly losing altitude when it feels like he is flying straight ahead. Keeping his faith only in the truth of his instruments will save him from disaster.

---

82 Joseph Stowell, IBID, p. 43
83 Joseph Stowell, IBID, p. 43

The thing that will get you through the tough times of suffering and trial is keeping your faith in God through trusting the truth of His Word when your feelings may lead you to believe Satan's lie that it doesn't pay to serve God. Dr. Stowell's insight is worth another quote from him.

> "Sometimes in pain we discount the value of truth by saying, 'But, I only know God's truth from the neck up; it doesn't make sense in my heart.' That's OK! It's what you know from your neck up that will enable you to keep your head up. In time, it will make sense in your heart. Just don't let go of the truth." [84]

Trust in the good process of God

The good Person of God is working His good purpose in your life through His good process. This wonderful passage of Scripture, Romans 8:28, reveals to us several facets of this process that will strengthen you when you are suffering.

- Becoming like Christ is a continuous process. "God 'works' all things together . . ." "Works" is a present active verb meaning that this is an ongoing process. On the assembly line at the Mercedes Benz plant, they do not take a huge chunk of steel and put a Mercedes Benz insignia on it. It is a long process involving thousands of steps to produce the finished product. So it is with God's process of making you like Christ. So you must believe in God's process and trust Him to bring you through your suffering.

- Becoming like Christ is also an inclusive process. It includes "all things," whether they be pleasurable or painful, whether they be desirable or undesirable to you. It is true that pain is part of the process. In the context of this eighth chapter of Romans, you see that you are "presently suffering" (verse. 18) and you live in a world that is "groaning" (verse. 22), and you personally are "groaning" (verse 23) as you await the completion of God's plan.

---

[84]   Joseph Stowell, IBID, p. 45

It is unfortunately true that when things are going well and life is pleasurable, your spiritual eyes and ears tend to be dull, and you do not see your need of God.

- Becoming like Christ is a process that is empowered and directed by God Himself. It is so much easier to take the suffering when you know that it is God Himself who is working in every detail of your life as a believer. Like the disciples on the stormy Lake Galilee, you tend to see the foreboding evil (a ghost) in the wind and the waves instead of Jesus Christ walking calmly on the waves of your storm.[85] Think of Joseph, sold into slavery by his brothers. Wrongfully accused and imprisoned, and after spending many years in God's refining process, he could say to his brothers *"But as for you, you meant evil against me; but God meant it for good, in order to bring it about as it is this day, to save many people alive."* [86]

- Becoming like Christ is also a process with an eternal perspective. Romans 8:28-29 is not saying, "Just keep your chin up! Everything will turn out OK in this life!" No, rather, it is proclaiming that God is working all things for your ultimate good as a believer. It is your eternal good that God has in mind; not just your temporal good. Kent Hughes comments:

"It really is true! God does cause everything that happens to us (even the evils inflicted by others, even the presently inexplicable disappointments) to work out for every believer's eternal good. This immense confidence rests on the certainty of our redemption which began before time with God's foreknowledge and will end beyond time with our glorification." [87]

Are you experiencing some suffering right now? Are you facing some extreme trial that you can't comprehend? Have you been struggling for a long time because of some tragedy in your life out of which you have not been able to make any sense?

---

[85] Mark 6:45-52
[86] Genesis 50:20; Also for the complete story, read Genesis 39-47
[87] Kent Hughes, Romans, Righteousness From Heaven (Crossway Books, Wheaton, Illinois, 1991) p. 167-168

Are you able to recommit yourself to Christ Jesus today with the assurance that God's promise to you in Romans 8:28-29 is eternally true? Will you renew your trust in the Heavenly Father who is working in all things for your eternal good? Whether the circumstances of your life right now are painful or pleasurable, can you submit to His loving purpose in your life which will lead eventually to your glory in heaven?

Philippians 1:6 says: ". . . being confident of this very thing, that He who has begun a good work in you will complete it until the day of Jesus Christ . . ."

Some study questions for your reflection

1. Some people assume that suffering or difficulty is a sign that God is judging a person for some sin or disobedience. Is this always a valid conclusion? 1 Peter 3:13-17; 1 Corinthians 11:27-32.
2. Romans 8:28 is God's rock solid promise. Is this His promise to all people? To whom is this promise given? Can you rightfully claim this promise? On what basis can you claim this promise?
3. Is everything that God sends into your life, or allows to happen in your life, in and of itself good? Study Romans 8:18-25. In this passage Paul is speaking about the groaning of creation under God's judgment as a result of man's sin. When will we, as believers, ultimately be delivered from the results of this general judgment?
4. What are three reasons that we, as believers, can trust God to keep His promise in Romans 8:28?
5. When a believer is suffering, what does Satan seek to have him believe about God? Job 1:22.
6. What attributes (characteristics) of God's nature give us the assurance that He is trustworthy even when we are going through troubles? Psalm 31:19; 34:8; Romans 8:31-39; John 3:16.
7. As we live out our time on this earth, what is God's purpose for us as believers? Romans 8:2.

8. How does difficulty and suffering fit into this purpose of God? What kind of response from us is needed in order to have these tough times mold us for God's purpose? 1 Peter 5:6-11; Job 13:15.
9. What response from us as believers does James command? James 1:2-4. How is this possible for us as believers?

Chapter 11

The Holy Spirit In Your Life

While Jesus was physically present here on earth, He walked and talked with His disciples. They became so attached to Him that they could not bear the thought of being separated from Him. As He rapidly approached the time when He would suffer and die on the cross for our sins, He began to share with them that He would soon leave them and return to the Heavenly Father. In John 13:33, Jesus announced His soon departure.

> *Little children, I shall be with you a little while longer. You will seek Me; and as I said to the Jews, 'Where I am going, you cannot come'. . .*

This announcement by Jesus upset the disciples. Peter questioned Jesus about where He was going (John 13:36). Jesus' response to Peter's question seems somewhat evasive. He does not tell him at this point that He is returning to His Father. Instead of answering Peter's question, Jesus turns the focus on Peter, questioning whether he would really lay down his life for his Master (John 13:36-38). Then in the next chapter of John, Jesus explains that He will be returning to His Father (John 14:28).

The disciples were disturbed by Jesus' talk about leaving them. Jesus promised them that He would return to receive them to Himself and they would always be with Him. This promise is of great comfort to all believers as we think of our glorious future home. John 14:1-3 records the words of Jesus when he says:

> "Let not your heart be troubled; you believe in God, believe also in Me. In My Father's house are many mansions; if it were not so, I would have told you. I go to prepare a place for you. And if I go and prepare a place for you, I will come again and receive you to Myself; that where I am, there you may be also . . ."

Another companion like Jesus

Jesus then announced to His followers that the Father was going to send another companion to be with them. He would leave them but they would not be alone. The promised Holy Spirit would be with them constantly. John 14:16-18 clearly says that they would not be orphaned from God because the promised Holy Spirit would be in their lives and Jesus Himself would return to them someday.

> *I will pray the Father, and He will give you another Helper, that He may abide with you forever - the Spirit of truth, whom the world cannot receive, because it neither sees Him nor knows Him; but you know Him, for He dwells with you and will be in you. I will not leave you orphans; I will come to you.*

The word translated *"another"* is from a Greek word that means *"another of the same kind."* The Holy Spirit would be Someone just like Jesus Himself who would take the place of Jesus and would do the work of Jesus in their lives. This Spirit of truth that Jesus promised is the Third Person of the Trinity, having the same essence of Deity as Jesus. The Holy Spirit is perfectly one with the Father as Jesus is one with the Father.

The word *"Helper"* can also be translated as *"Comforter," "Advocate"* or *"Counselor."* The original word in the Greek language is the word *"Paracletos"* which literally means *"one called alongside to help."*[88] As a believer in Jesus Christ, you have the Holy Spirit to be your constant companion. Like Jesus, He will never leave you nor forsake you. He is present in your life to direct you according to the teachings of Jesus Christ Himself. As Jesus made clear to the disciples, the Holy Spirit always lifts up the Son. One of the Spirit's jobs is to remind you of what Jesus teaches in the Word.[89]

The Holy Spirit, the One who convicts

John 16:7-11 records the words of Jesus:

> *Nevertheless I tell you the truth. It is to your advantage that I go away; for if I do not go away, the Helper will not come to you; but if I depart, I will send Him to you. And when He has come, He will convict the world of sin, and of righteousness, and of judgment: of sin, because they do not*

---

[88] The MacArthur Study Bible, Word Bibles, Nashville, London, Vancouver, Melbourne, page 1614.
[89] John 14:26; 15:26

> *believe in Me; of righteousness, because I go to My Father and you see Me no more; of judgment, because the ruler of this world is judged.*

The assigned work of the Holy Spirit is to convict us of sin, righteousness and judgment. Only as the Holy Spirit does His convicting work in your life and mine are we able to see our need of a Savior. Until such time as the Holy Spirit opens our eyes, we will continue to believe that we are able to get to heaven on our own. Only as the Holy Spirit convinces us of our sinfulness and our lost condition before God are we brought to repentance and faith in Jesus Christ. In 1 Corinthians 2:13-14, the apostle Paul speaks of this blindness of the natural man who does not know Christ.

> *These things we also speak, not in words which man's wisdom teaches but which the Holy Spirit teaches, comparing spiritual things with spiritual. But the natural man does not receive the things of the Spirit of God, for they are foolishness to him; nor can he know them, because they are spiritually discerned.*

The Holy Spirit convicts of sin, opening up the spiritual eyes of an unbeliever to convince him of his hopeless lost condition. The Holy Spirit brings a person to the conviction that he is in great danger of the eternal punishment as he is judged by God for his sins. The Holy Spirit reveals Jesus Christ as the only Savior for sin. Until this illuminating work of the Holy Spirit occurs in the unbeliever's mind and heart, he is blind to his sinful and lost condition.

The baptism and filling of the Holy Spirit

Confusion exists in the minds of many Christians over the baptism and the filling of the Holy Spirit. Some denominations and some Christian teachers have created this confusion by failing to distinguish biblically between these terms. You can avoid the confusion by clearly understanding the terms *"baptism"* and *"filling"* as they apply to the ministry of the Holy Spirit.

- **The baptism by the Holy Spirit.**

The baptism by the Holy Spirit is referred to in the Bible in two aspects. First, it occurs in reference to the historical event known as Pentecost. Secondly, it refers to the action of the Holy Spirit in a person who comes to faith in Jesus Christ.

1. First, the baptism by the Spirit at Pentecost. Pentecost means "fifty days" and is the historical date of the founding of the church at Jerusalem. At that time the Holy Spirit was given to the church in fulfillment of the promise of Jesus to send another Helper like Himself.

When Jesus was baptized by John, the Baptist, John prophesied the baptism of the Spirit. In Matthew 3:11, we read:

> *I indeed baptize you with water unto repentance, but He who is coming after me is mightier than I, whose sandals I am not worthy to carry. <u>He will baptize you with the Holy Spirit</u> and fire.*

Jesus ascended to the Father forty days after His death. Just before His ascension, as recorded in Acts 1:4-5, Jesus refers to John's prophecy. He instructs His followers to remain in Jerusalem until this prophecy was fulfilled.

> *And being assembled together with them, He commanded them not to depart from Jerusalem, but to wait for the Promise of the Father, "which," He said, "you have heard from Me; for John truly baptized with water, but you shall be baptized with the Holy Spirit not many days from now."*

We read of the fulfillment of this promise in Acts 2. Something special happened ten days after the ascension of Jesus. The prophet, Joel's prediction of the unique outpouring of the Holy Spirit is fulfilled (compare Joel 2:28-32 with Acts 2:15-21). So the baptism by the Spirit, according to Scripture itself, was the historical event of Pentecost when the Holy Spirit was poured out upon the believers who waited in Jerusalem as Christ commanded them to do.

2. Now to the second aspect of the term "baptism by the Spirit." Paul, the apostle, used the term "baptized" by the Spirit only once, in 1 Corinthians 12:13.

> *For by one Spirit we were all baptized into one body—whether Jews or Greeks, whether slaves or free—and have all been made to drink into one Spirit.*

This Scripture teaches that every true believer has been baptized by the Holy Spirit into the body of Christ. If you are part of Christ's body, the universal church, you got into that body by baptism (immersion) into the Holy Spirit. This is how a sinner, who is dead spiritually, is regenerated (made alive spiritually). He is baptized (immersed) by the Holy Spirit and he is, from then on, a part of the body of Christ. In fact, Paul emphatically declared in Romans 8:9 "*. . . if anyone does not have the Spirit of Christ, he is not His.*"

Some Christians will ask you "Have you been baptized by the Spirit?" Because of their failure to understand the teaching of the Bible, they mean something far different than the Bible teaches. They have been taught that the baptism by the Spirit is a special experience often distant in time from one's salvation experience. They believe there is a second level experience when you come to a total surrender to the lordship of Christ and Christ baptizes you then by the Holy Spirit. Those who teach this view usually also believe, as they have been taught, that this experience will be accompanied by "speaking in tongues." If you are ever asked "Have you been baptized by the Spirit?" your reply should be, "Yes, I was baptized by the Spirit when I trusted Christ as my Savior and Lord."

- **The filling of the Holy Spirit.**

The apostle Paul uses another term in Ephesians 5:18-21. Here he teaches us that all of us as believers are to be continually being filled by the Holy Spirit.

> *And do not be drunk with wine, in which is dissipation; but be filled with the Spirit, speaking to one another in psalms and hymns and spiritual songs, singing and making melody in your heart to the Lord, giving thanks always for all things to God the Father in the name of our Lord Jesus Christ, submitting to one another in the fear of God.*

The filling of the Holy Spirit is the experience of every believer who maintains a constant walk with the Lord Jesus Christ. The term "filling" should not be thought of as the possession of a portion of the Spirit at one time and perhaps a greater portion at another time. You are not a quarter full or half full of the Spirit, as if the Holy Spirit can be portioned out to you. As a believer, you always have all of the Holy Spirit. What Paul is speaking about is the "control" that the Holy Spirit has in your life as a believer. Is He being allowed by you to control your life completely? In other words, does the Holy Spirit possess all of you as a believer?

Paul says in Ephesians 4:30: ". . . *do not grieve the Holy Spirit of God, by whom you were sealed for the day of redemption."* We grieve the Holy Spirit when we allow any unforsaken and unconfessed sin to remain in our lives. In this way, we block the control of the Holy Spirit as we refuse to heed His conviction of our sin. Until we are willing to confess or own up to our sin, we are resisting the work of the Holy Spirit in our lives. Remember to practice 1 John 1:9 constantly in your life. *"If we confess our sins, He is faithful and just to forgive us our sins and to cleanse us from all unrighteousness."*

Paul uses another term to speak of this experiential "filling" by the Holy Spirit in Romans 8:5. He refers to *"living by the Spirit"* in contrast to *"living by the flesh."* As believers, we are constantly to be living by or walking by the Spirit.

"How can I be filled by the Holy Spirit?" you ask. Each day, as you begin your day, recognize that you cannot live the Christian life by your own strength. Therefore, recognize your need of the Holy Spirit to control you completely. Make certain that you have confessed any sin known in your life. Then invite the Holy Spirit to take complete charge of your life.

Another question you may be asking, "But, how do I know that I am filled by the Holy Spirit?" By faith! The Lord commands every believer to be filled by the Spirit. The normal way of life for every believer is to be controlled by the Holy Spirit continually. If God commands you to be filled or controlled by the Holy Spirit, do you think He will withhold this experience from you? Take a look at 1 John 5:14-15.

> *Now this is the confidence that we have in Him, that if we ask anything according to His will, He hears us. And if we know that He hears us, whatever we ask, we know that we have the petitions that we have asked of Him.*

Do you see God's promise? He will answer any prayer that we pray according to His will. If God commands you to be filled or controlled by His Holy Spirit, it is clear that this is His will for you. So if you are clean from any unconfessed sin, and you ask for the Lord Jesus to fill you with His Holy Spirit, will He do it? Of course, He will.

"But, what if I don't feel like it?" The filling or control of the Holy Spirit does not depend upon your feelings. It is a matter of faith. If it were dependent upon your feelings, you would not be able to be filled by the Spirit when you are going through difficult circumstances.

The fruit of the Holy Spirit

The evidence that you are controlled by the Holy Spirit is not whether or not you speak in tongues, as some teach. Nor is it that you are in possession of some other gift of the Holy Spirit. In fact, much damage can be done to the cause of Christ by someone who seeks to use his gifts and abilities when he is not being controlled by the Holy Spirit.

The evidence of the filling of the Holy Spirit is that your life begins to bear fruit. When Jesus was teaching His disciples about false teachers, He said clearly, "Therefore, by their fruits, you will know them."[90] Paul teaches that the Holy Spirit produces fruit in the life of the believer who is abiding in Christ. In John 15:1-8, Jesus teaches us about this fruitfulness that comes from abiding in Christ Jesus.

> *I am the true vine, and My Father is the vinedresser. Every branch in Me that does not bear fruit He takes away; and every branch that bears fruit He prunes, that it may bear more fruit. You are already clean because of the word which I have spoken to you. Abide in Me, and I in you. As the branch cannot bear fruit of itself, unless it abides in the vine, neither can you, unless you abide in Me.*
>
> *I am the vine, you are the branches. He who abides in Me, and I in him, bears much fruit; for without Me you can do nothing. If anyone does not abide in Me, he is cast out as a branch and is withered; and they gather them and throw*

---

[90] Matthew 7:20

> them into the fire, and they are burned. If you abide in Me, and My words abide in you, you will ask what you desire, and it shall be done for you. By this My Father is glorified, that you bear much fruit; so you will be My disciples.

The apostle Paul teaches that the Christian who is walking obediently under the control of the Holy Spirit will produce the fruit of the Spirit. The fruit of the Spirit is clearly listed by Paul in Galatians 5:22-25:

> But the fruit of the Spirit is love, joy, peace, longsuffering, kindness, goodness, faithfulness, gentleness, self-control. Against such there is no law. And those who are Christ's have crucified the flesh with its passions and desires. If we live in the Spirit, let us also walk in the Spirit.

It is important for you as a follower of Jesus Christ to allow the Holy Spirit to produce a Christ-like life in you. The description of the fruit of the Spirit given by the apostle Paul aptly describes our Savior, Jesus Christ. It is God's purpose to make you more and more like Jesus Christ. Don't be discouraged if you fail to produce fruit all of the time. Gradually you will grow to be Christ-like as you seek to submit yourself to the control of the Holy Spirit.

The gifts of the Holy Spirit

The apostle Paul was concerned that no one would be ignorant or uninformed about the gifts of the Holy Spirit. In 1 Corinthians 12:1 he wrote: *"Now concerning spiritual gifts, brethren, I do not want you to be ignorant: . . ."* [91]

As Paul continued to write, he is teaching that the Holy Spirit of God gives some special ability or special enablement to every believer which he is to use for the good of the whole body of believers. 1 Corinthians 12:4-11 further explains this important area of serving the Lord with our Spirit-given gifts.

> *There are diversities of gifts, but the same Spirit. There are differences of ministries, but the same Lord. And there are*

---

[91] The word "gifts" does not actually occur in the Greek text but is inserted by the translators because this is what is implied in the context. Actually, the apostle is speaking about "spirituals" or things that pertain to the Holy Spirit.

diversities of activities, but it is the same God who works all in all. But the manifestation of the Spirit is given to each one for the profit of all: for to one is given the word of wisdom through the Spirit, to another the word of knowledge through the same Spirit, to another faith by the same Spirit, to another gifts of healings by the same Spirit, to another the working of miracles, to another prophecy, to another discerning of spirits, to another different kinds of tongues, to another the interpretation of tongues. But one and the same Spirit works all these things, distributing to each one individually as He wills.

Note some of the major ideas that Paul teaches us about spiritual gifts in this passage.

1. There are diversities of gifts, but all are given by the same Holy Spirit. The gifts that are given to one believer may be different from that given to another believer. God has a different purpose and plan for each believer as he relates to and serves the Lord in the body of Christ.

2. Whatever gifts you have received from the Spirit are intended for the benefit or profit of all believers. When God gives you gifts, He doesn't intend that you simply use them upon yourself. Neither are they intended to bring you glory. Rather they are to glorify God by enhancing the body of believers.

3. The gifts that are bestowed upon each believer individually are not given because of our personal desires or ambitions. They are not given in response to our pleading before God but they are divinely distributed according to the sovereign will of the Spirit.

The apostle Paul lists some spiritual gifts in 1 Corinthians 12:8-10, and he expands the list in verses 28-31. Here he makes it abundantly clear that no gift is for all believers, for the Holy Spirit has chosen to gift us all differently. Nor does any believer possess all of the gifts.

And God has appointed these in the church: first apostles, second prophets, third teachers, after that miracles, then gifts of healings, helps, administrations, varieties of tongues. Are all apostles? Are all prophets? Are all teachers? Are all

> *workers of miracles? Do all have gifts of healings? Do all speak with tongues? Do all interpret? But earnestly desire the best gifts. And yet I show you a more excellent way.*

Paul continues on in 1 Corinthians 13 to talk about the *"more excellent way."* It is the way of love. Apparently, even in Paul's day, there was controversy over the use of spiritual gifts. Certainly there is controversy today also. Some churches practice "tongues speaking" today. Others believe that this was intended as a sign gift, limited to the early church as the written text of the Bible was being revealed to the apostles. Controversy and differences exist when it comes to the role of "miracles" today. Other areas of difference occur in regards to "words of knowledge" and "prophecies." Paul further deals with the gifts of tongues and prophecy, in 1 Corinthians 14, where he also gives some guidelines of how the gift of tongues was to be exercised in the gathered assembly. To deal with these controversial differences about the gifts of the Spirit is beyond our purpose. [92]

My opinion is that it is not honoring to the Lord when we allow differences of understanding on issues like spiritual gifts to cause disunity among brothers and sisters in Christ. It is healthy to have congregations where we hold to different views on non-essential issues as long as we do not allow our different views to build walls of separation within the larger body of Christ.

It is also my opinion that the Holy Spirit did not intend to give us a complete list of spiritual gifts as He inspired the apostle Paul to write. In Romans 12:6-8, Paul gives another list as he writes to the church at Rome. In this list, he does not even mention the gifts of tongues or miracles.

> *Having then gifts differing according to the grace that is given to us, let us use them: if prophecy, let us prophesy in proportion to our faith; or ministry, let us use it in our ministering; he who teaches, in teaching; he who exhorts, in*

---

[92] My personal position is that the sign gifts (tongues, miracles by miracle workers, prophecies in the sense of words of knowledge or new revelations from the Lord) are not valid for today. Tongues were a sign for unbelievers (1 Corinthians 14:22). "Tongues" was the ability to speak in a language spoken in the world given miraculously by the Holy Spirit, without having learned that language by normal learning processes. For further study of this subject, see MacArthur Study Bible, IBID.

> *exhortation; he who gives, with liberality; he who leads, with diligence; he who shows mercy, with cheerfulness.*

The apostle Peter also writes about spiritual gifts in 1 Peter 4:10-11. He is not inspired by the Holy Spirit to list the gifts other than to single out *"speaking as the oracles of God"* and *"ministering"* or serving.

> *As each one has received a gift, minister it to one another, as good stewards of the manifold grace of God. If anyone speaks, let him speak as the oracles of God. If anyone ministers, let him do it as with the ability which God supplies, that in all things God may be glorified through Jesus Christ, to whom belong the glory and the dominion forever and ever. Amen.*

Peter's primary concern is to encourage each believer to understand the gift or gifts the Holy Spirit has given and to use those gifts under the enablement of God. The ultimate goal of each of us is to glorify God through Jesus Christ.

As a believer, always seek to follow the Holy Spirit's leading in your life. He will empower you to do the will of God and to become more and more like Jesus Christ. He will empower your witness for Christ as you seek to be God's instrument to share the "good news" with others. Acts 1:8 reminds us of the promise of Jesus just before He ascended to the Father:

> *But you shall receive power when the Holy Spirit has come upon you; and you shall be witnesses to Me in Jerusalem, and in all Judea and Samaria, and to the end of the earth.*

Some study questions for your reflection

1. Who is the Holy Spirit according to Scripture?
2. How do we know that the Holy Spirit is God? What did Jesus mean when He said that the Father would send "another Helper" like Himself?
3. What does the word "Helper" (Greek word is "Paracletos") mean to you as you seek to understand the ministry of the Holy Spirit in your life?

4. What does the "baptism by the Holy Spirit" mean scripturally?
5. What does it mean to be "filled with the Holy Spirit" as Paul speaks of this in Ephesians 5:18?
6. How can we hinder, grieve or disrupt the work of the Holy Spirit in our lives? When we fall into this sin against the Holy Spirit, how can we once more know the control of the Holy Spirit? What steps must we take as believers?
7. Why does the Holy Spirit give "gifts" unto us as believers?
8. Do you have any idea at this point in your life what gift(s) the Holy Spirit has given you? If so, how are you using those gifts to benefit the body of believers?[93]

---

[93] Seek help from the pastor of your church to discover the gifts given you as a believer.

Chapter Twelve

You Are A Manager For The Lord!

The word "stewardship" has long been used in Christian circles to refer to our responsibility to manage the resources that God has entrusted to us. A steward is one who is placed in charge of the possessions of another. The Scriptures teach us that God owns all things and He rules over all things. The Psalmist speaks of this in Psalm 24:1-2.

> *The earth is the LORD's, and all its fullness, The world and those who dwell therein. For He has founded it upon the seas, And established it upon the waters.*

God is the Creator and Sustainer of all that exists, including all human beings. By right of creation, He is our owner. Life itself is a gift from God. As the apostle Paul declared in his speech to the Athenians on Mars Hill, God is the "... *Lord of heaven and earth, (Who) does not dwell in temples made with hands. Nor is He worshiped with men's hands, as though He needed anything, since He gives to all life, breath, and all things.*"[94]

Jesus taught that we are servants who are responsible for managing everything He has entrusted into our hands. In one of His parables recorded in Matthew 25:14-30, Jesus shares this concept of faithful stewardship of God's gifts.

> *For the kingdom of heaven is like a man traveling to a far country, who called his own servants and delivered his goods to them. And to one he gave five talents, to another two, and to another one, to each according to his own ability; and immediately he went on a journey. Then he who had received the five talents went and traded with them, and made another five talents. And likewise he who had received two gained two more also. But he who had received one went and dug in the ground, and hid his lord's money.*

Probably years went by before the day of reckoning.

> *After a long time the lord of those servants came and settled accounts with them. So he who had received five talents*

---

[94] Acts 17:24-25

came and brought five other talents, saying, 'Lord, you delivered to me five talents; look, I have gained five more talents besides them.' His lord said to him, 'Well done, good and faithful servant; you were faithful over a few things, I will make you ruler over many things. Enter into the joy of your lord.' He also who had received two talents came and said, 'Lord, you delivered to me two talents; look, I have gained two more talents besides them.' His lord said to him, 'Well done, good and faithful servant; you have been faithful over a few things, I will make you ruler over many things. Enter into the joy of your lord.'

What about the servant who had received only one talent?

Then he who had received the one talent came and said, 'Lord, I knew you to be a hard man, reaping where you have not sown, and gathering where you have not scattered seed. And I was afraid, and went and hid your talent in the ground. Look, there you have what is yours.' But his lord answered and said to him, 'You wicked and lazy servant, you knew that I reap where I have not sown, and gather where I have not scattered seed. So you ought to have deposited my money with the bankers, and at my coming I would have received back my own with interest. So take the talent from him, and give it to him who has ten talents. For to everyone who has, more will be given, and he will have abundance; but from him who does not have, even what he has will be taken away. And cast the unprofitable servant into the outer darkness. There will be weeping and gnashing of teeth.'

In biblical times a talent was measured by weight. Therefore a talent of gold would be more valuable than a talent of silver. Whether silver or gold, a talent was a large amount of money. Many scholars interpret this parable as speaking of more than merely money. They feel that Jesus was speaking about all of the possessions we have, including our money, our natural abilities and our God-given spiritual gifts. God has given us the responsibility of faithfully using our lives for His kingdom purposes and to bring benefit and glory to God. God only holds us accountable for that which He has given us. Note that the servant who received two talents is commended equally with the servant who was given five talents. They are both commended for their faithfulness. Paul, the apostle, says in 1 Corinthians 4:2,

"*Moreover it is required in stewards that one be found faithful.*" The unprofitable servant is judged because he simply buried his talent and wasted his opportunities. As an unfaithful servant, he is judged by the Lord and banished into outer darkness.

Who owns your life?

As a believer and follower of the Lord Jesus, you are not the owner of your life. Not only does God have claim upon your life as your Creator; He also owns your life because He has redeemed you from your sinful lost condition. As the apostle Peter states,

> *. . . you were not redeemed with corruptible things, like silver and gold . . . but with the precious blood of Christ, as a lamb without blemish and without spot.* [95]

The apostle Paul also teaches us that we belong to Christ and are to recognize that Christ Jesus owns all rights to our lives. 1 Corinthians 6:19-20 states:

> *Or do you not know that your body is the temple of the Holy Spirit who is in you, whom you have from God, and you are not your own? For you were bought at a price; therefore glorify God in your body and in your spirit, which are God's.*

Three areas of stewardship

Life is a trust from God. He entrusts in at least three areas: time, talents and treasures. If we view our lives as a trust from God, this will determine how we live our lives. We will not live our lives for our selfish endeavors but for the glory of God. We will not view this life as most important but rather we will see this life as being preparatory for eternity. We as believers are simply pilgrims [96] here on earth who have our citizenship in heaven. We are foreigners with "green cards" here on earth.

Management of our time

Paul speaks of the urgency of managing our time in Ephesians 5:15-16: "*See then that you walk circumspectly, not as fools but as*

---

[95]   1 Peter 1:18-19
[96]   1 Peter 2:11ff

wise, redeeming the time, because the days are evil." We are to be "redeeming the time" while we live here on this earth.

In the New Testament, two different words are used to refer to time. In the Greek language, one word is "chronos" that speaks of the duration of time. The word "chronometer" comes from this word which is in essence a watch that measures time in minutes, hours, days, months and years (Matthew 2:7; Luke 4:5). Another word is "kairos," the word used by the apostle Paul in Ephesians 5. It has an entirely different meaning. This word speaks of time in the sense of opportunity. The emphasis is upon the unique periods of time in your life that are specific opportunities that God is placing in your pathway.

Paul is not telling us to crowd as much activity and as much work into each day as we possibly can. He is not telling us that we should never rest or sit idly as we meditate and enjoy the roses along life's pathway. In fact, the more we pack our days and weeks with frantic activity, the more we may be disobeying his command to "redeem the time."

If you read the next verse in this passage of Scripture, you will find that Paul is linking "redeeming the time" with knowing and doing the will of God. In verse 17, he says, *"Therefore do not be unwise, but understand what the will of the Lord is."* It is always God's will that we live godly lives that honor Him. It is always God's will that we love one another. It is always God's will that we place priority on those things that have eternal significance.

A dad who is spending all his time at work, focusing his energies on his career, is not redeeming the opportunities he has to be a father to his kids. A mom who is so consumed with her career and her house chores that she has no time for her children is not redeeming the opportunities to mold her children for the Lord.

How are you as a believer in Christ Jesus using your opportunities of sharing the gospel with your neighbors? Are you alert in showing the love of Christ to the people you contact every day? We redeem our time by keeping our priorities straight.

In Matthew 24:42-44, Jesus speaks to us about His second coming, the time when He will return to this earth, and time as we know it will come to an end. He says:

> *Watch therefore, for you do not know what hour your Lord is coming. But know this, that if the master of the house had known what hour the thief would come, he would have watched and not allowed his house to be broken into. Therefore you also be ready, for the Son of Man is coming at an hour you do not expect.*

By watching for His return, Jesus does not mean that we are to be constantly looking up into the sky to see if He is returning at this very moment. Rather, he is speaking of watching carefully how we are living our lives, so that whenever He comes, we are living for His glory. Then we will not be caught off guard no matter when He comes again. We will be pleasing God always in the way in which we live our lives.

Life on this earth is temporary in nature. Therefore we are to live proper godly lives as we wait for Christ's return for us. We can waste quantities of time that could be used more wisely to make for quality of time. If I spend my hours watching television and then excuse the fact that I have not had time to study my Bible, I am simply deceiving myself. If I choose to spend my time on my own selfish pleasures and claim I have no time to spend with my son, I am deceiving myself. Allow the Holy Spirit to guide you to redeem the time. A converted Hindu who had been given a Bible and a clock said, "The clock will tell me how time goes, and the Bible will tell me how to spend it." [97]

Management of our talents and Spirit-given abilities

The Bible teaches that the Holy Spirit gives to every believer at least one gift. These gifts are mentioned in various places in the New Testament. However, there is question whether the New Testament gives a complete listing of spiritual gifts, as each list differs from the others. The list of spiritual gifts in 1 Corinthians 12:28-31 is different from the list in Romans 12:6-8.

> *1 Corinthians 12:28-31 says: "And God has appointed these in the church: first apostles, second prophets, third teachers, after that miracles, then gifts of healings, helps, administrations, varieties of tongues. Are all apostles? Are*

---

[97] George Sweeting, Who Said That, (Moody Press, Chicago, 1994) p. 425

> all prophets? Are all teachers? Are all workers of miracles? Do all have gifts of healings? Do all speak with tongues? Do all interpret? But earnestly desire the best gifts. And yet I show you a more excellent way."

> Romans 12:6-8 says: "Having then gifts differing according to the grace that is given to us, let us use them: if prophecy, let us prophesy in proportion to our faith; or ministry, let us use it in our ministering; he who teaches, in teaching; he who exhorts, in exhortation; he who gives, with liberality; he who leads, with diligence; he who shows mercy, with cheerfulness."

Besides spiritual gifts that are given to believers by the Holy Spirit, God has also gifted each of us with natural abilities and talents. Even non-believers ought to recognize that their abilities and talents are from God.

It is often difficult to distinguish where a spiritual gift begins and a talent or ability ends. They are often blended in character. For example, a non-believer may have a talent for public speaking and when he becomes a Christian, the Spirit of God gives him a gift of prophecy or preaching. A person may have an excellent singing voice but he or she is given a gift of mercy which enhances his or her natural ability with spiritual impact.

As a believer in Jesus Christ, you must identify your spiritual gifts given to you by the Holy Spirit. Then endeavor to use those gifts under the power of the Holy Spirit to serve the Lord and His church. 1 Peter 4:10-11 speaks about this matter of using our gifts for the glory of God.

> As each one has received a gift, minister it to one another, as good stewards of the manifold grace of God. If anyone speaks, let him speak as the oracles of God If anyone ministers, let him do it as with the ability which God supplies, that in all things God may be glorified through Jesus Christ, to whom belong the glory and the dominion forever and ever. Amen.

But, you ask, how can I know what my gifts are?

- First, pray that the Lord will show you what gifts He has given to you by His Spirit.

- Experiment by trying different ministries as the Lord gives you opportunity.

- Seek help from others who will be honest with you as they share what they believe that you do especially well.

- Your pastor may have some spiritual gifts test that you can take to help you discover your spiritual gifts.

- What ministries do you enjoy and feel fulfilled doing? The areas where you are gifted to serve will produce the most satisfaction and joy as you use your gifts.

- Be concerned that the fruit of the Spirit (Galatians 5:19-21) is displayed in your use of your Spirit-given gifts. Only as the fruit of the Spirit is present will your gifts be effectively used for the glory of God.

The management of our treasures

Jesus spoke frequently about our treasures and how we use them. He exhorted His followers to be laying up treasures in heaven rather than accumulating them on earth. Matthew 6:19-21 records some of His powerful words on this subject.

> *Do not lay up for yourselves treasures on earth, where moth and rust destroy and where thieves break in and steal; but lay up for yourselves treasures in heaven, where neither moth nor rust destroys and where thieves do not break in and steal. For where your treasure is, there your heart will be also.*

We often say "if your heart is in it, your treasure will be there also." Jesus reversed this thought and said "where your treasure is, there your heart will be." Therefore, if we want our hearts to be set on eternity, then we need to place our treasures there also.

Paul, the apostle, warns Timothy against greed as he writes to him in 1 Timothy 6:6-10.

> *Now godliness with contentment is great gain. For we brought nothing into this world, and it is certain we can carry nothing out. And having food and clothing, with these we shall be content. But those who desire to be rich fall into temptation and a snare, and into many foolish and harmful lusts which drown men in destruction and perdition. For the love of money is a root of all kinds of evil, for which some have strayed from the faith in their greediness, and pierced themselves through with many sorrows.*

The Bible never says that money is evil. Rather money is seen as good in that it is useful for many things. The book of Proverbs often speaks of planning ahead for a day of need and exhorts us not to be lazy and non-productive with our lives. Paul says that it is *"the love of money that is a root of all kinds of evil."* It is greed that leads us to many other forms of evil in order to achieve prosperity upon which we have placed our hearts' desires.

Paul does not castigate the rich man but, rather, he exhorts him about how he uses his money. He is to use his wealth to serve others. In so doing he will be laying up treasures in heaven. 1 Timothy 6:17-19 speaks plainly about how we are to handle our wealth.

> *Command those who are rich in this present age not to be haughty, nor to trust in uncertain riches but in the living God, who gives us richly all things to enjoy. Let them do good, that they be rich in good works, ready to give, willing to share, storing up for themselves a good foundation for the time to come, that they may lay hold on eternal life.*

Is tithing necessary for New Testament believers?

Certainly tithing is taught for the Jewish people in the Old Testament. But is it necessary for us as believers today to tithe?

When the Jewish people were living under Moses' law, they were commanded to give a tithe (a tenth) of all of their gain to the Lord. The first tenth of all they earned was to be given back to the Lord. For example, Leviticus 27:30, 32, established this tithe principle for them.

> *And all the tithe of the land, whether of the seed of the land or of the fruit of the tree, is the Lord's. It is holy to the Lord . . . And concerning the tithe of the herd or the flock, of whatever passes under the rod, the tenth one shall be holy to the Lord.*

The last prophet of the Old Testament, Malachi, chastises the Jewish people for robbing God in not giving their tithes and offerings to God. He also challenges them to bring their tithes and offerings into God's storehouse and see how God will bless them for their obedience to Him. Malachi 3:6-12 exhorts Israel to return to obedience to the Lord in their tithing of their possessions.

> *"For I am the Lord, I do not change; therefore you are not consumed, O sons of Jacob. Yet from the days of your fathers you have gone away from My ordinances and have not kept them. Return to Me, and I will return to you," says the Lord of hosts.*

> *"But you said, 'In what way shall we return?' "Will a man rob God? Yet you have robbed Me! But you say, 'In what way have we robbed You?' In tithes and offerings. You are cursed with a curse, for you have robbed Me, even this whole nation. Bring all the tithes into the storehouse, that there may be food in My house, and try Me now in this," says the Lord of hosts, "If I will not open for you the windows of heaven and pour out for you such blessing that there will not be room enough to receive it. "And I will rebuke the devourer for your sakes, so that he will not destroy the fruit of your ground, nor shall the vine fail to bear fruit for you in the field," says the Lord of hosts; and all nations will call you blessed, for you will be a delightful land," says the Lord of hosts.*

In the New Testament Gospels, we find that Jesus rebuked the Pharisees harshly for their hypocritical life-styles. In Matthew 23:23, we find some of Jesus' words of reprimand to the Pharisees.

> *Woe to you, scribes and Pharisees, hypocrites! For you pay tithe of mint and anise and cummin, and have neglected the weightier matters of the law: justice and mercy and faith.*

> *These you ought to have done, without leaving the others undone . . .*

We need to be careful in interpreting what Jesus said to them. Some take this passage to mean that Jesus told them that they ought not to tithe. Jesus actually commended them for tithing but He told them that their tithing was not sufficient. While they ought to tithe, He says, they ought not to neglect much more important things such as justice, showing mercy to others and faithfulness. It seems to me that Jesus was putting His stamp of approval upon tithing, while cautioning them not to view tithing as the completion of all their duties in serving the Lord. It is incomprehensible that a Jew would begin to give less than a tithe (that which the law required of him) now that he had come to know Christ Jesus as his Messiah and Savior. The tithe is a good beginning point in our financial stewardship as followers of Jesus Christ.

Some New Testament principles of financial stewardship

The apostle Paul taught some principles to the church at Corinth that raised the bar for our giving to God beyond the point of obligation to tithe. In 1 Corinthians 16:1-4, he spoke to them about the way in which they were to give an offering to the believers in Jerusalem who were in desperate need through a famine that had inflicted their land. He says to them:

> *Now concerning the collection for the saints, as I have given orders to the churches of Galatia, so you must do also: On the first day of the week let each one of you lay something aside, storing up as he may prosper, that there be no collections when I come. And when I come, whomever you approve by your letters I will send to bear your gift to Jerusalem. But if it is fitting that I go also, they will go with me.*

In 2 Corinthians 8:1-5, he shared with them how some other believers in other places had been setting an example by their sacrificial and willing giving to the needs of others.

> *Moreover, brethren, we make known to you the grace of God bestowed on the churches of Macedonia: that in a great trial of affliction the abundance of their joy and their deep poverty*

abounded in the riches of their liberality. For I bear witness that according to their ability, yes, and beyond their ability, they were freely willing, imploring us with much urgency that we would receive the gift and the fellowship of the ministering to the saints. And not only as we had hoped, but they first gave themselves to the Lord, and then to us by the will of God.

Then Paul shared with them some principles to guide them in their giving to the Lord as he wrote to them in 2 Corinthians 9:6-11.

But this I say: He who sows sparingly will also reap sparingly, and he who sows bountifully will also reap bountifully. So let each one give as he purposes in his heart, not grudgingly or of necessity; for God loves a cheerful giver. And God is able to make all grace abound toward you, that you, always having all sufficiency in all things, may have an abundance for every good work. As it is written:

"He has dispersed abroad, He has given to the poor; His righteousness endures forever."

Now may He who supplies seed to the sower, and bread for food, supply and multiply the seed you have sown and increase the fruits of your righteousness, while you are enriched in everything for all liberality, which causes thanksgiving through us to God.

Now, let's summarize the principles that guide us in our proper financial stewardship to our God.

- ♦ The tithe is a good beginning point in our giving. The tithe is the Lord's. Do not be guilty of robbing God, like Israel did.

- ♦ The first day of the week is to be a day of a stewardship check-up in our worship of God. I Corinthians 16:2. It is to be a day when we ask, "How has God blessed me financially this past week?" Then we are to give back to God *"in keeping with our income."* This means that we are to give according to the measure in which God has blessed us. Proportionate giving is taught in the Scriptures. This means that we ought to give beyond the tithe as God blesses us with abundance.

The story is told of a young man who made a covenant with God that he would tithe all that the Lord gave to him. He consistently tithed the small amount of money that he earned in his teen years. He went off to college and continued to tithe. Then he became a very successful businessman and began to think about the huge amount of money that he was tithing to the Lord. So he went to his pastor and said, "You know I can no longer afford to tithe. I would like you to pray with me to God and have Him remove my covenant to tithe." The wise elderly pastor said to him, "Well, I cannot do that, my friend. But what I will do is to ask God to reduce your income so that you will be able to afford to tithe." How easy it is for us to become earth centered and greedy with the possessions that God entrusts to us.

♦ Our giving ought to be free-will giving from our hearts. In 2 Corinthians 8:12, Paul says, *"For if there is first a willing mind, it is accepted according to what one has, and not according to what he does not have."* We must have a willing spirit in our giving. In 2 Corinthians 9:7, Paul says that we must give what we have decided in our hearts to give. We must not give simply because we feel compelled to give. If we feel only a compulsion to give, this indicates our need of a changed heart, so that we might give unselfishly as Jesus gave.

♦ Our giving must be with a joyful spirit. *"God loves a cheerful giver"* (2 Corinthians 9:7). Someone has said that this means God loves a hilarious giver. Do you gain great delight from giving for the Lord's purposes?

♦ Our giving should follow the pattern of the farmer. In 2 Corinthians 9:6, Paul reminds us that the farmer must sow an adequate amount of seed in order to reap a good harvest. If he skimps on the seed, he will get a skimpy harvest. But if he sows generously, he will reap generously. So it is with our giving to God. If God knows that He can trust us to use our possessions for His glory and for His good purposes, then He will give us more.

♦ Our giving ought to flow from a thankful heart. As Paul concludes chapter nine of 2 Corinthians, he emphasizes God's great gift to us. He says, *"Thanks be to God for His indescribable gift."* This is referring to Jesus Christ, God's Son, whom God the Father gave for our salvation.

♦ Become a generous, giving follower of Jesus Christ. The more we give to the Lord's work, the more eternal treasure we are laying up in heaven.

God's promises to good stewards

God does not promise prosperity to every believer as some preachers say. But God promises to provide for His faithful people. Let's review some of God's promises to those who faithfully use their financial blessings for His glory and honor.

♦ God promises to provide for those who seek first His kingdom and His righteousness. In the context of Matthew 6:33, Jesus Christ promises to take care of the needs of all who trust Him and seek to serve Him. *"But seek first the kingdom of God and His righteousness, and all these things shall be added to you."* We are not worry about what we are to wear or what we are going to eat. As we keep our priorities in order and trust our Lord and Savior, He will provide for all our daily needs.

The apostle Paul speaks about God's gracious provision for all of our needs in Philippians 4:19 where he says, *"And my God shall supply all your need according to His riches in glory by Christ Jesus."* We need to understand this promise in the context or we may distort Paul's message. In verses 10-13, we read:

> *But I rejoiced in the Lord greatly that now at last your care for me has flourished again; though you surely did care, but you lacked opportunity. Not that I speak in regard to need, for I have learned in whatever state I am, to be content: I know how to be abased, and I know how to abound. Everywhere and in all things I have learned both to be full and to be hungry, both to abound and to suffer need. I can do all things through Christ who strengthens me.*

Paul is affirming his trust in the Lord, which enables him to *"do all things through Christ who strengthens me."* The Lord enabled him to endure each circumstance in his life, whether being hungry or full. When the Lord in His wisdom does not see fit to provide financial abundance, He will give the strength to make it through the time of trial.

- Through the prophet, Malachi, God promised Israel that He would bless them by *"throwing open the floodgates of heaven and pour out so much blessing that you will not have room enough to receive it."* Certainly God was promising to bless their crops and their herds and make their nation a blessing and a delightful land.[98] However, we ought to be careful about interpreting this promise to Israel as a promise of great financial blessing to all of His redeemed people. The blessings of giving to the Lord and to His work in a generous way enrich us in many ways besides physical and financial blessings. God will reward us with a sense of peace and well-being for doing His work in helping others. He also has promised us rewards in heaven for laying up treasure in heaven.

- God promises to care for us and to provide enough of everything in our lives, as we faithfully and joyfully give to Him and to His eternal work. Read 2 Corinthians 9:6-11 again. Note God's promise is to "increase your store of seed," in other words to give you more seed to scatter for Him. He also promises to *"enlarge the harvest of your righteousness."* In other words, He will make your life count for His righteous purposes and for His kingdom's sake. Sometimes, you will wonder if you can give any more when you have responded generously to many good purposes. In verse 8, He promises to *"make all grace abound toward you, that you, always having all sufficiency in all things, may have an abundance for every good work."* Verse 11 says, *"while you are enriched in everything for all liberality . . ."*

- Your life will be lived as a life of thanksgiving to God. You will be thankful to the Lord and others will give thanks to God for you and your generosity in helping God's people (2 Corinthians 9:11-15).

One of the greatest challenges of your life as a believer is to allow the Holy Spirit to make you a generous person who delights in investing your treasures in heaven. The natural tendency of the old nature is to make us greedy rather than generous. We are by nature 'this-world-minded' rather than 'eternally-minded'. We tend to grasp onto our treasures rather than give them to Jesus. However, when the Lord returns and all these earthly things are

---

[98] Malachi 3:10-12

destroyed, only what we have invested in heaven will remain.[99] So keep your heart always on heaven and live your time on this earth with eternity's values in clear view.

Some study questions for your reflection

1. What is the basic meaning of stewardship? What are some examples that Jesus gives us in the Gospels (Matthew, Mark, Luke and John) of our stewardship before God?
2. What is the main requirement of being a good steward of the Lord? 1 Corinthians 4:2.
3. What are two reasons that God holds a claim on your life? In the light of the Scriptures, what is the reason you cannot claim to 'own' your life?
4. What are the three areas in which you need to recognize God's claim upon your life?
5. What does it mean to "redeem the time"? Ephesians 5:15-16. Does this have anything to say about priorities in your life? How can you apply this principle more effectively in your life right now?
6. As you see yourself at this point in your life, what special gifts and abilities do you believe God has given you? Why do you believe these are gifts from God? In what ways can you find further help to identify your spiritual gifts and abilities?
7. What does Jesus mean by "laying up treasures in heaven"? How does Paul tell Timothy that those who are rich can do this? Matthew 6:19-21; 1 Timothy 6:17-19.
8. What do you believe the Scriptures teach about your financial stewardship before the Lord? What does God require of us as believers in the use of our possessions?
9. Do you have any struggles in your life in this matter of giving to the Lord? What are some of the principles in the New Testament toward which you believe the Lord would have you work in order to be more obedient to the Lord in financial stewardship?

---

[99] 2 Peter 3:10-13

10. In regards to the stewardship of your life before God, what do you think you will wish you had done in this life when you arrive home in heaven? Is this not what you should prayerfully seek to do now?

Chapter Thirteen

Your Life's Purpose Until You Arrive Home!

Life without Jesus Christ may be happy and productive but it is a meaningless existence. Life before you knew Christ Jesus had no real eternal purpose. The person who has not experienced the new birth in Jesus Christ has nothing to look forward to except an eternity separated from God forever. The unbeliever stumbles through this life, seeking to find something worthwhile and meaningful. He seeks it in material possessions, in pleasure, in popularity and notoriety, or in his career "success." But as far as eternity goes, it is all meaningless and empty. Solomon, the writer of Ecclesiastes expresses this in a powerful way as he says: *"Vanity of vanities . . . all is vanity."* [100]

Without God in your life, you are simply living your life as if there is no God and no existence after this life. The only sensible view of life, if there is no God, is "eat, drink and be merry, for tomorrow you die!" Get all the 'gusto' you can out of life here and now because life here is all there is for which to live.

However God is! And God has created everything for His glory and His eternal purpose. Every human being is made with an eternal soul. Only as one comes to faith in Jesus Christ and finds new life in Christ does he find true meaning and purpose. That purpose is to bring glory to God! Revelation 4:11 says:

> *You are worthy, O Lord, to receive glory and honor and power; for You created all things, and by Your will they exist and were created.*

In Romans 11:33-36, Paul shares a wonderful doxology that expresses this thought of God's purpose for all of His creation.

> *Oh, the depth of the riches both of the wisdom and knowledge of God!*
> *How unsearchable are His judgments and His ways past finding out!*
> *"For who has known the mind of the Lord?*

---

100 Ecclesiastes 1:2

> *Or who has become His counselor?"*
> *"Or who has first given to Him*
> *And it shall be repaid to him?"*
> *For of Him and through Him and to Him are all things,*
> *to whom be glory forever. Amen."*

You are a citizen of heaven

As a believer in Jesus Christ, you have a new life that is abundant and full. It has purpose and meaning because of who you are in Christ. You are a new creature in Christ Jesus with an eternal hope and an eternal future in heaven. The New Testament teaches us that the believer in Jesus Christ is a citizen of heaven and he is no longer just a citizen of the world. You still must live in this world but you do not belong to the world anymore. You belong to God and are destined for heaven. Paul, the apostle, speaks of this heavenly citizenship in Ephesians 2:19 when he says *"Now, therefore, you are no longer strangers and foreigners, but fellow citizens with the saints and members of the household of God . . ."*

Before you accepted Christ into your life, you were a foreigner to God's kingdom. You were outside of the family of God and were not a citizen of heaven. But now that you have Christ in your life and are owned by God as His child, you are a stranger or foreigner to this world. Your citizenship is in heaven and you are waiting to go home someday where you belong. Paul writes to the Philippian church in Philippians 3:18-21:

> *For many walk, of whom I have told you often, and now tell you even weeping, that they are the enemies of the cross of Christ: whose end is destruction, whose god is their belly, and whose glory is in their shame— who set their mind on earthly things. For our citizenship is in heaven, from which we also eagerly wait for the Savior, the Lord Jesus Christ, who will transform our lowly body that it may be conformed to His glorious body, according to the working by which He is able even to subdue all things to Himself.*

The more you become like Jesus Christ, the less you will feel like you fit into this world anymore. As Peter expresses it in 1 Peter 2:9-12:

But you are a chosen generation, a royal priesthood, a holy nation, His own special people, that you may proclaim the praises of Him who called you out of darkness into His marvelous light; who once were not a people but are now the people of God, who had not obtained mercy but now have obtained mercy.

Beloved, I beg you as sojourners and pilgrims, abstain from fleshly lusts which war against the soul, having your conduct honorable among the Gentiles, that when they speak against you as evildoers, they may, by your good works which they observe, glorify God in the day of visitation.

Set your mind on heaven

Every day of your life is to be lived with heaven in your sights. Your mind is to be set on heavenly things, that is, upon things that have lasting significance. Paul, the apostle, writes in Colossians 3:1-4:

If then you were raised with Christ, seek those things which are above, where Christ is, sitting at the right hand of God. Set your mind on things above, not on things on the earth. For you died, and your life is hidden with Christ in God. When Christ who is our life appears, then you also will appear with Him in glory.

There is a common expression that I have heard repeatedly since I was very young. It says: "He is so heavenly minded that he is no earthly good." If a Christian is so removed from life in this world that he does nothing to seek to serve others and to reach others with the gospel, then that saying is true. The key (in the verses above) is where we set our minds. We are to be involved in this world while not becoming like the world in our values, our goals and our way of living. We cannot be of any earthly good in serving our Lord Jesus unless our minds are set on heavenly things.

The theme of this chapter is: what do the Scriptures teach us about setting our minds on heavenly things?

Live for the glory of God

In everything that God has done for us in rescuing us from our sin and redeeming us through Jesus Christ, He has done for His glory. As He works His eternal plan including each believer in that plan, it is all for His glory. He has placed His Holy Spirit in each believer, guaranteeing his eternal inheritance in heaven, all for His own glory. Read Ephesians 1:1-14, noting the phrase *"to the praise of His glory"* and other comparable ideas. God has plainly made each human being for His own purposes and every time a person comes to know Jesus Christ, it is for the praise of His glory.

Live a godly life

In the context of Colossians 3, Paul teaches us that *"setting our minds on heavenly things"* means that we allow the life of Christ to be lived out through us. It involves "putting to death" whatever belongs to the old sinful nature and clothing ourselves with the clothes of the new nature.

The purpose of God is to make us more and more like Jesus Christ while we are living out our lives here on this earth.[101] We are to be conformed to the image of Jesus Christ. So we must put to death all those evil deeds such as *"sexual immorality, impurity, lust, evil desires and greed, which is idolatry,"* all those things for which *"the wrath of God is coming."* [102] Paul continues by telling us that we must *"rid ourselves of all such things as these: anger, rage, malice, slander, and filthy language from your lips. Do not lie to one another . . ."* These things are no longer to be part of our lives because we have put off the old nature and have put on the new nature in Christ Jesus.[103] Fortunately, God helps us! If we try to do it – put off the old nature – in our own strength, we'll likely fail. God will help us do anything He wants us to do. We just need to ask Him and then lean heavily upon Him for His power.

In putting on the new nature, we also must rely on Him. We are to allow the Holy Spirit to produce the fruit of the Spirit in our

---

[101] Romans 8:29
[102] Colossians 3:5-6
[103] Colossians 3:8-10

lives continually. Note the similarity of Colossians 3:12-17 to Galatians 5:22-23 and Ephesians 5:18-20. We are to be living our lives like Jesus Christ. We are to be living examples to our world of our Lord and Savior, Jesus Christ. To be like Jesus Christ in this world is God's purpose for us. In so doing, we will shine as lights in this darkened world. Philippians 2:14-16 summarizes this aspect of God's will in our lives that leads to a life that is not lived in a purposeless way.

> *Do all things without complaining and disputing, that you may become blameless and harmless, children of God without fault in the midst of a crooked and perverse generation, among whom you shine as lights in the world, holding fast the word of life, so that I may rejoice in the day of Christ that I have not run in vain or labored in vain.*

Involve yourself in the work of God

Everything we do is to be done for the praise and glory of our great God. Whether we are working on a secular job, going to school, enjoying some leisure, or living in our home relationships, we are to be doing all in such a way as to glorify God. Paul writes in 1 Corinthians 10:31-33:

> *Therefore, whether you eat or drink, or whatever you do, do all to the glory of God. Give no offense, either to the Jews or to the Greeks or to the church of God, just as I also please all men in all things, not seeking my own profit, but the profit of many, that they may be saved.*

♦ **Be a Great Commandment Christian**

Love is the mark of the true Christian. Jesus said, *"By this all will know that you are My disciples, if you have love for one another"* (John 13:35). The 'Great Commandment' is given to us by the Lord Jesus as it is recorded for us in Mark 12:30-31. When Jesus was asked which of the commandments was the most important, He answered:

> *"And you shall love the Lord your God with all your heart, with all your soul, with all your mind, and with all your strength." This is the first commandment. And the second, like it, is this: "You shall love your neighbor as yourself." There is no other commandment greater than these.*

If you seek to love others with the love of Christ, you will fulfill the will of God in your life. Love that is Christ-like is acting according to the best interest of the other person. Therefore, loving others with Christ-like love may mean that you will confront others about their behavior. You will do what is best for the other person's eternal good. Paul the apostle defines this kind of love in 1 Corinthians 13. Verses 4-8 read:

> *Love suffers long and is kind; love does not envy; love does not parade itself, is not puffed up; does not behave rudely, does not seek its own, is not provoked, thinks no evil; does not rejoice in iniquity, but rejoices in the truth; bears all things, believes all things, hopes all things, endures all things. Love never fails . . .*

- ### Be a Great Commission Christian

Every one of us as Christ's followers is to take seriously the 'Great Commission' that Christ gave to us. Just before Christ ascended to heaven, He gave His disciples an assignment. We find it recorded for us in its most complete form in Matthew 28:18-20.

> *And Jesus came and spoke to them, saying, "All authority has been given to Me in heaven and on earth. Go therefore and make disciples of all the nations, baptizing them in the name of the Father and of the Son and of the Holy Spirit, teaching them to observe all things that I have commanded you; and lo, I am with you always, even to the end of the age."*

This task of sharing the "good-news" with others is not to be done only by "professionals" - pastors, evangelists and missionaries. We do not hire pastors for our churches to do all the work of God. Each of us as Christ's followers is given the task of serving Christ, as we seek to bring others to Jesus Christ. When Jesus was praying to the Heavenly Father just before His death on the cross, He prayed that the Father would sanctify us through His truth and that He would keep us from the evil one. Then he prayed *"As You sent Me into the world, I also have sent them into the world"* (John 17:18).

Why did the Father send His Son, Jesus, into this world? Why did He come to our messy, sin-filled world anyway? Jesus said in John 6:37-40:

> *"All that the Father gives Me will come to Me, and the one who comes to Me I will by no means cast out. For I have come down from heaven, not to do My own will, but the will of Him who sent Me. This is the will of the Father who sent Me, that of all He has given Me I should lose nothing, but should raise it up at the last day. And this is the will of Him who sent Me, that everyone who sees the Son and believes in Him may have everlasting life; and I will raise him up at the last day."*

Jesus plainly declared that "... *God so loved the world that He gave His only begotten Son that whoever believes in Him should not perish but have everlasting life... God did not send His Son into the world to condemn the world, but that the world through Him might be saved.*"[104] 2 Peter 3:9 shows us the heart of God. He "... *is longsuffering toward us, not willing that any should perish but that all should come to repentance.*"

Christ has given each of His followers a mission to fulfill. That mission is to do our utmost to bring others to know Jesus Christ so they will be recipients of His salvation. Our mission is to bring as many with us to heaven as we can. How can we do that? We must seek, through the power of the Holy Spirit, to share the gospel message with all who will listen. As Paul, the apostle expresses it to the Corinthian church, one plants the seed and another waters it, but it is God who makes it grow.[105] There is no greater thrill than to see another person come to trust Jesus Christ as Savior and Lord and to help that person mature as a believer. Talk with your pastor about getting involved in some evangelism training so that you may grow in your ability to share the gospel clearly and effectively with those who are still among the lost and wandering.

Look for the return of your Savior and Lord

The more Christians suffer, the more they long for the second coming of our Lord and Savior, Jesus Christ. The New Testament Scriptures are filled with promises of the return of the Lord Jesus to gather those who are saved to Himself in heaven. As Jesus ascended into heaven, the disciples were standing there gazing into the skies in wonderment. Two men clothed in white apparel

---

[104] John 3:16-17
[105] 1 Corinthians 3:5-9

spoke to them and said *"Men of Galilee, why do you stand gazing up into heaven? This same Jesus, who was taken up from you into heaven, will so come in like manner as you saw Him go into heaven"* (Acts 1:11).

These Scriptures speak of the coming of Jesus Christ to bring the world to an end. At the end of time, a great world ruler will come upon the scene that does not honor God. He is known in the Bible as the Anti-Christ. At God's appointed time, Christ Jesus will bring judgment upon all of the world powers ruled by the Anti-Christ and He will usher in His kingdom rule. This time of righteous rule is known as the millennium, meaning a "thousand years." Then there will be a final battle against Satan and his rebel forces, followed by the final judgment of unbelievers who will be banished to the "lake of fire" forever, along with Satan and all evil spirits. Revelation 20 gives a capsule view of these events.

Ultimately, Jesus Christ will make a new heaven and a new earth where righteousness will reign forever and ever. We will be freed from the burden and the effects of sin and evil. Jesus will reign as King of kings and Lord of lords forever and ever. Read Revelation 21 and 22 to get a picture of this final estate we often refer to as heaven.

There are many views that are held by sincere Christians as to the details of the end times and the second coming of Jesus Christ. It is not our purpose in this book to get into the details and the debates about which is the right view. However, it is clear that Jesus wants all of His followers to be ready for His return whenever it happens. In Matthew 24:42-44 we read the words of Jesus to His followers as He spoke to them about the future events and the end of the age.

> *Watch therefore, for you do not know what hour your Lord is coming. But know this, that if the master of the house had known what hour the thief would come, he would have watched and not allowed his house to be broken into. Therefore you also be ready, for the Son of Man is coming at an hour you do not expect.*

How can we be ready for His return? Christ is not telling us to "watch" for His return by walking around with our heads in the air, looking up into the skies to see if He is coming. He is speaking about watching how we live our lives. A thief catches his victim off guard. We must not be caught off guard. We are to be walking in this world in such a way that we will not be ashamed when He comes. He will find us living for His glory and living for eternal purposes.

A favorite passage of mine is Titus 2:11-14. Here Paul, the apostle, gives a challenge to Titus and to all believers, calling us to look and long for His return.

> *For the grace of God that brings salvation has appeared to all men, teaching us that, denying ungodliness and worldly lusts, we should live soberly, righteously, and godly in the present age, looking for the blessed hope and glorious appearing of our great God and Savior Jesus Christ, who gave Himself for us, that He might redeem us from every lawless deed and purify for Himself His own special people, zealous for good works.*

Home at last!

"And, Lord, help us to end well." This statement was frequently heard at the close of Dr. William Culbertson's public prayers. He was president of Moody Bible Institute from 1948 to 1971 and a faithful servant whose prayer was answered. He ended well. A worthwhile spiritual exercise is to ponder how we will end our lives. [106]

As a follower of Jesus Christ, the ultimate goal is to be with the Lord Jesus in heaven's glory. There is no greater prize than to be welcomed home by Jesus and to hear Him say, *"Well done, good and faithful servant."*[107]

There is an old familiar story of a missionary returning home for the last time after serving for more than forty years on the mission field. He had labored faithfully for the Lord with his wife. They had often struggled with lack of financial support and frequently failed to see much result of their efforts. A wonderful band welcomed the ship on which they returned to New York harbor, and throngs of people were at the dock. But it was not to welcome them home. President Theodore Roosevelt was also on the ship and the rest of the passengers were delayed in getting off the ship until the president made his departure to cheering of the

---

[106] From Warren Wiersbe's publication, "Prokope", April - June, 1998
[107] Matthew 25:21,23

throngs. Other passengers, including the missionaries, were then allowed to exit.

The missionary was feeling sorry for himself as no one was there to greet him and his wife. After forty years of service, there was no one to thank them, to honor them. As he was bemoaning his lonely departure from the ship, the Lord Jesus reminded him, "Just remember, you are not home yet!" [108]

When we struggle to persevere in trusting and serving the Lord Jesus, it is good for us to remember that we are not home yet.

So walk with the Lord Jesus! Let Him be Lord and Master of your life. Seek the joy of following Him and obeying Him. Trust Him when the way is not clear and what He is doing is not plain. Know that *"all things work together for good to those who love God, to those who are the called according to His purpose."*[109] Seek to continue to grow in the Lord Jesus through studying the Scriptures and through learning to walk intimately with Jesus in your prayer life. He will show you the way that you shall go. The rewards will be eternally wonderful and you will find that you have not wasted your life.

Some study questions for your reflection

1. How does God give purpose and meaning to life? Why is there no meaning to life if God doesn't exist or if we leave God out of our lives?
2. God tells us that He made all things for His glory! Revelation 4:11; Ephesians 1; etc. What do you think it means for you as a Christian to bring glory to God?
3. You are a citizen of heaven. How should this affect your life here on earth, in this temporal world?
4. A life that is lived for God's purposes is the eternally meaningful life. What does it mean to live a godly life? What are we not to do? What are we to do? How can you know what pleases God or displeases Him?

---

108   Source of this story is unknown to me.
109   Romans 8:28-29

5. What is God's work in this world? If you are going to involve yourself in God's work, what will that mean in your life?
6. What is the Great Commandment that Jesus gave us? Why is this so crucial in living for Christ? In what ways does "love" for others aid in your witness for Christ?
7. What is the Great Commission that Jesus has given us? How does God want you to be involved in helping fulfill the mission that He has assigned to us? In what ways can you practically fulfill this aspect of God's will in your life?
8. Jesus Christ is coming back for you someday. What happens if you die before the second coming of Jesus Christ? Study 1 Thessalonians 4:13-18.
9. What does "watching" for Jesus' return mean? How can you be ready if He should come today? Are there some practical changes that the Lord would have you make in your life in order to be ready for His return?
10. Are there some things in your life right now to which you must say "NO", in order to be more prepared for Jesus' return? Titus 2:11-14.
11. What is the ultimate goal of the disciple of Jesus Christ? How do you want to finish your life? Are there some changes you need to make in order to finish your life well?

ISBN 141202024-7